The Craigmont Story

Dedication: To Katharine.

Acknowledgement

My background in the British Columbia mining communities of Pioneer and Bralorne helped me to understand the language of mining, but it took the patience and the understanding of a great many people to help bring the Craigmont operation to life.

William "Bill" Diment receives my greatest praise for he has served in many capacities. As manager of Craigmont during its final years, he was able to open many doors which might otherwise have remained closed. His enthusiasm and his patience in reading through several drafts of this book can only be considered above and beyond the call of duty. I must also thank Anthony J. "Tony" Petrina and the directors of Craigmont Mines Ltd. Without their faith and their financial support, the Craigmont story would be no more than a few pages.

John Simpson, Lucile McDiarmid, Robert Baird, John Roberts and others played key roles in the development of the mine and this book. They deserve a vote of thanks.

Special thanks must also go to the staff and the directors of the British Columbia Museum of Mining and the Nicola Valley Museum-Archives. Their frank and constructive criticism helped to create a better product.

                                                    Murphy Shewchuk.

The Craigmont Story

Murphy Shewchuk

hancock
house

ISBN 0-88839-980-4

Catalog in Publication Data

Shewchuk, Murphy.
The Craigmont story

Bibliography: p.
ISBN 0-88839-980-4

1. Craigmont Mines Ltd. — History. 2. Copper mines and
mining — British Columbia — Nicola Valley — History. 3.
Nicola Valley (B.C.) — History. I. Title.
HD9539.C7C72 1983   338.2'743'09711   C83-091335-1

Edited by Brett Westcott
Typeset by Elizabeth Grant in Chelmsford
    on an AM Varityper Comp/Edit
Production, Layout & Cover Design by Eva Raidl
Design & Layout by Dorothy Forbes
Production Assistant Jill Gibson
Printed in Canada by Friesen Printers

Published by

HANCOCK HOUSE PUBLISHERS LTD.
19313 Zero Ave., Surrey, B.C. V3S 5J9
HANCOCK HOUSE PUBLISHERS INC.
1431 Harrison Avenue, Blaine WA. 98230

Table of Contents

Introduction

Mining is an industry that deals with a finite resource. The life of a mine is determined by the size and the nature of the orebody and the ability of men and women to extract the minerals profitably. *The Craigmont Story* is the story of the life of a mid-twentieth century British Columbia copper mine. This is a story of the formation of the orebody beneath the earth's surface, how it was discovered, how it was mined and how the land is being returned to cattle range. Most importantly, this is the story of the people of Merritt, the Nicola Valley and British Columbia who were part of Craigmont from its first hesitant beginnings until there was no longer any ore left to mine.

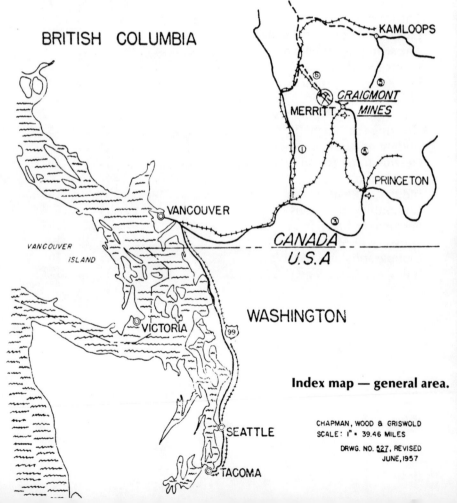

Index map — general area.

CHAPMAN, WOOD & GRISWOLD
SCALE: 1" = 39.46 MILES
DRWG. NO. 527, REVISED
JUNE, 1957

Located near Merritt, British Columbia

The Craigmont Mine property is located on the southeast slopes of the Promontory Hills in south-central British Columbia about nine miles (15 kilometres) from Merritt and 180 miles (200 kilometres) northeast of Vancouver. Elevations in the area range from 1,865 feet (565 metres) at the Nicola River, to 2,400 feet (732 metres) at the plant site and to 5,689 feet (1,734 metres) at the top of Promontory Hill. The region is dry with an annual precipitation of about 12 inches (30 centimetres); temperatures range from about -22 to 100 degrees Fahrenheit (-30 to 39 degrees Celsius).

Craigmont pit near completion of open-pit mining in 1967.
Craigmont photo

Craigmont Operated for more than Two Decades

After more than twenty years of operation, 1982 marked the final year of copper production at the Craigmont mine. Craigmont became a successful mine when it commenced operations in 1961. It continued to be a successful mine through periods of poor copper markets, labor unrest, government policy changes and unprecedented inflation. In an achievement that is unusual in the world of business, Craigmont ended as a successful operation.

Craigmont's success can be measured in the copper produced, the profits made and, most importantly, the people who benefited from the mine and the secondary industry it helped to support.

Craigmont Produced a Billion Pounds of Copper

During Craigmont's lifetime as a copper producer, it added over 947 million pounds (426 million kilograms) of copper to the world's marketplace. The mine grossed over $450 million in sales. Production costs included approximately $112 million paid in wages to employees. Craigmont had net earnings over its two-decade lifetime of $115 million and it paid shareholders $107 million in dividends. The federal and the provincial governments received $74 million in direct taxes and in royalties. In addition to direct taxes, the company paid sales taxes on goods and on services while its employees paid income taxes on their wages and on their salaries.

During its operation, Craigmont also spent $8 million on outside exploration in search of another orebody.

5,000 Men and Women Worked at Craigmont

However, corporations make many achievements that do not appear on the pages of an annual report or on the bottom line of a balance sheet. Approximately 5,000 people were employed at

8

Craigmont during the period between 1946, when its predecessor Pinecrest Gold Mines Ltd. was formed, and 1983 when Craigmont's mining operation was terminated.

Craigmont Mines Ltd. was made up of living, breathing people — as many as 660 people were employed at one time during the peak years of operation — and the multitude of personalities involved in every facet of the mining operation gave the company a character all its own. Craigmont was alive.

On the job, these people contributed much to improve mining technology at Craigmont and, as a result, to improve mining technology world-wide. British Columbia had a history of copper mining in the late 1800s, but by the 1950s, it had ceased to be a significant copper producer. Craigmont was the mine that led British Columbia's re-emergence as a major copper-producing region. Partly because of Craigmont's success, a number of other large copper mines were developed which turned British Columbia into a significant source of copper for world markets.

Ray Archer on modified John Deere. January 1972.
Craigmont photo

First Modern Open-Pit Copper Mine

Craigmont can also take credit for starting British Columbia's first modern, large-scale open-pit mine. Even in the early 1960s, Craigmont was able to mine at rates of up to 50,000 tons (45,000 tonnes) per day which provided a continuous mill feed of 5,560 to 6,670 tons (5,000 to 6,000 tonnes) per day and a stockpile that helped to carry the mine during the transition to underground mining.

The same enthusiasm and innovation led to the introduction of an underground mining system known as sublevel caving, a method originally developed in Sweden, but previously unknown and untried in North America. In its underground operation, Craigmont spurred the development of trackless diesel and hydraulic machinery. When the equipment was not available to suit their needs, Craigmont's engineers and tradesmen modified existing equipment or they designed and fabricated new equipment and new mining procedures.

The entire mining system worked well as it equalled and often surpassed other copper mines around the world.

The Multiplier Effect Created Additional Jobs

The people who were employed at Craigmont also significantly contributed to the life of the community and the province. Craigmont was a major force in the growth of the economy of Merritt and of the Nicola Valley. The salaries and the wages of hundreds of employees, through the multiplier effect, provided jobs in a wide variety of secondary and service industries. Craigmont employees also significantly contributed their own time and effort. Two of Merritt's mayors, several aldermen and numerous hospital, school board and community service group members worked at the mine at various points in their careers.

Countless people worked at Craigmont before they then went on to use their talents in other mines and in other industries throughout North America. One former Craigmont engineer, Tom

Waterland, has become a Member of the Legislative Assembly and a cabinet minister in British Columbia.

For some people, Craigmont was a job, but for others Craigmont was a way of life. Regardless of their reasons for being there, it took people from all walks of life to make the Craigmont mine a successful operation.

P & H Shovel and Euclid truck at open-pit 1961.

Craigmont photo

Craigmont Has Its Beginnings

Neil H. McDiarmid Formed Craigmont in 1951

Neil H. McDiarmid was a lawyer with his soul in British Columbia's mining industry. He began his law practice in the early 1920s at Likely, British Columbia, in the heart of the famed Cariboo gold fields. McDiarmid and his young family moved to Vancouver in 1929 where he continued to practise law and to maintain his lifelong interest in mining ventures.

It was during the post-World War Two mining boom when the predecessor to the Craigmont company was formed with gold interests in the Kettle Valley, south of Beaverdell, British Columbia. Pinecrest Gold Mines Ltd. (Non-Personal Liability) was incorporated September 2, 1946, by McDiarmid and his close associates, Hartley Davis and T.C. "Tom" Botterill. With gold prices fixed at $35 (U.S.) per ounce while mining costs continued to rise, new gold mining ventures proved unattractive and little activity took place on behalf of Pinecrest Gold Mines Ltd.

McDiarmid and Botterill acquired a large low-grade multi-mineral property near Princeton, British Columbia, which they also placed in the name of Pinecrest Gold Mines Ltd. Unfortunately, they were unable to raise sufficient capital to proceed and the properties were abandoned.

On July 5, 1951, McDiarmid reorganized the company and changed the name to Craigmont Mines Ltd. (Non-Personal Liability).

Highland Valley Boom Sparks Renewed Interest in Promontory Mountain

The early 1950s was a period of extensive mineral claim staking in the Highland Valley, approximately 18 miles (30 kilometres) north of Merritt. The presence of copper in the Guichon Batholith had been known since the 1890s, but despite several attempts, the deposits did not support a mine. The industrial growth of the 1950s prompted a second look at these deposits. The demand for copper was growing and improvements in mining technology suggested the mining of large low-grade deposits could be viable.

The Highland Valley copper deposits were part of a broad belt of copper mineralization that extended from Lake Chelan in Washington State, through Princeton, the Nicola Valley, the Highland Valley and northwestward beyond Cache Creek.

The interest in the Highland Valley spilled over into the Nicola Valley and it prompted a number of prospectors to examine the old showings, including those on the Promontory Hills.

Among those showing an interest in the Nicola Valley area were Neil H. McDiarmid and Craigmont Mines Ltd. On August 17, 1954, Craigmont acquired 14 mineral claims which contained the Paystin and the Merchant groups on the Promontory Hills near Merritt.

Snowstorm and Compass Set Stage for Discovery

Harry D. Merrell was a Chilliwack-based contractor and prospector who made frequent trips to the Nicola Valley in the early 1950s. On one such trip, Merrell was doing some exploration work for Craigmont near Jackson Lake on the east slope of the Promontory Hills.

As winter closed in on the higher elevations, Merrell and another prospector, Martin Retan, left their crude camp and began working their way back down the mountain. During the last week before Christmas, 1954, Merrell and Retan staked a series of claims named

13

Merrell #1 to #8.

"It was on the 19th of December, 1954, when we staked that ground," recalled Merrell. "It was snowing pretty bad, making it hard to see. Martin Retan was going ahead of me and he started to circle to the right. I had to keep correcting him, trying to keep him in a straight line. When we were almost finished, we discovered that we had made a mess of the staking because something was attracting our compasses."

The snowstorm moved in as Merrell and Retan finished staking and it cut off access to the mountain which forced them to abandon their equipment until the following spring.

Lack of Money Delays Exploration

Despite Harry Merrell's suspicions of "something" in the Promontory Hills, the only thing this part of the mountain attracted was Merrell's compass. With no visible rock outcrop to sample and with little money available to diamond drill, most of the exploration activity continued some distance away on more promising showings near Jackson Lake.

A year later, December 20, 1955, Merrell sold his claims to Carmen R. Payie, who, along with Jack Stinson, had discovered fresh copper showings on the Paystin claims near Jackson Lake. In October, 1956, Craigmont Mines Ltd. acquired an option on the Merrell claims along with a number of others which increased the company's holdings on the east slopes of the Promontory Hills.

In April, 1955, Craigmont conducted special airborne magnetometer and scintillitometer surveys of the Craigmont mineral claims, but the results were inconclusive.

Soil-Sampling Kit Points to Mineral Deposit

R.E. Renshaw and Franklin Price explained in a story in the July, 1958, issue of "Mining World" how geochemical soil sampling was

14

used on the Promontory Hills:

"In 1956, Craigmont controlled a large area. The big question was where to diamond drill to find an orebody. While the general geology of the area was known, the lack of rock exposures necessitated a diamond-drill exploration program. But where to drill was the big question."

To compound this problem, Renshaw and Price also had to deal with a vast, overburden-covered area, seven small and apparently unrelated copper mineralization showings and limited time and money.

"After due consideration, it was decided that a soil testing survey, followed by a magnetometer survey, would be the best means of proving a favorable area as quickly as possible. The magnetometer has been used for many years and engineers have long appreciated its value in exploration of mineral deposits. Soil sampling, however, was a relatively new approach. After considerable research and several consultations with Dr. Harry V. Warren and Dr. R. Delavault, professors of geology at the University of British Columbia, the method decided to be the easiest and the most suitable was the rubianic acid technique perfected by them at the U.B.C."

Renshaw and Price laid out a grid on the mountain slope and they took soil samples just below the grass roots at 100-foot (30-metre) intervals. One gram of the soil sample was placed in a test tube and mixed with a strong acetic acid solution. The mixture was filtered and a drop of the solution was placed on a slip of rubianic acid reagent paper. The relative darkness of the resulting stain indicated the amount of copper present in the soil. The results were plotted on a map.

"As the work proceeded, the map took shape and it was seen that anomalies of copper concentration were long and narrow, parallel to the regional structure of the area, except one that was much wider. The completed soil sampling map outlined four anomalies, each about 200 feet (61 metres) wide except for the Merrell claim where the width was 1,200 feet (364 metres)."

"A magnetometer survey was later made over the area, using the same stations from which soil samples were obtained. The resulting magnetometer map confirmed the soil anomalies and they were almost identical in shape."

In April, 1956, Craigmont started a diamond drilling program on the east slopes of the mountain which was intended to explore the showings near Jackson Lake. To finance continued exploration, the directors of Craigmont — Raymond Collishaw, Neil H. McDiarmid, Earl Olts and Whitey Wilson — raised money through selling shares on the unlisted stock market in Vancouver.

Diamond Drill
Probes Anomaly

Rodney E. Renshaw also described the 1957 spring activities in the April 12, 1982, issue of "The Pacific Miner."

"We had arranged for some 2,000 feet (606 metres) of diamond drilling in the area of Jackson Lake. . .," wrote Ron Renshaw. "We had another little copper showing on the way up the steep, narrow jeep trail to the lake. After fighting to get the rig to Jackson Lake in the snow and mud, we found there was no way we could make it up the steep slope, so I said the heck with it. We unloaded the drill and put down two 100-foot (30-metre) holes."

"I also did something I wanted to do very much, drill the geochemical-magnetometer anomaly. . . This was the site of diamond drill number three."

Holes one and two were duds; Ron Renshaw left the diamond driller working on the site of hole three at the anomaly and he joined Raymond Collishaw and Earl Olts in Spokane, Washington, where they were discussing a uranium deal. Since Craigmont's money was running low, explicit instructions had been left with the driller to telephone every night with a progress report. As the diamond drill sank into the ground, so did the company's hopes and its bank account.

When the driller reached 200 feet (60 metres), he reported "a little malachite and some epidote present and the ground becoming more shattered." Though they were running low on cash, the directors decided to dig deeper into their pockets and to finance another 50 feet (15 metres) of drilling.

16

Hole Three Hits Ore

"Jerry was boiling over with glee when he called the next morning," wrote Renshaw. "He shouted over the phone: 'Ron, I took it down to 307 feet (93 metres). Gee! at that depth the core was loaded. I took the liberty of putting it down for another run. I knew you would do that yourself.'"

Hole three on the Merrell anomaly was really the first important discovery in the orebody. It was continued to a depth of 497 feet (152 metres) and had a continuous ore section of 337 feet (103 metres) which averaged 0.96 per cent copper and about 30 per cent iron. When the drillers stopped drilling, they were still in ore.

Although the ore grade was still not sufficient to warrant a mine, excitement was high. However, as holes four, five and six were drilled, the results did not improve and several important financial backers dropped out because they were convinced Craigmont would never become a mine.

Neil H. McDiarmid, a perpetual optimist, would not quit. "We mortgaged everything we had to keep going," said Neil's wife, Lucile. "Neil would not stop and I did not want to, either. He was an optimist. Thank God!"

In September, 1957, with all the McDiarmids's hopes and all their money riding on it, hole seven was drilled to a depth of 770 feet (235 metres). The hole averaged 1.91 per cent copper and 37 per cent iron for 645 feet (197 metres).

Hole seven was the clincher. Before the end of 1957, Craigmont acquired a total of 155 claims which covered 7,000 acres (2,800 hectares) on the slopes of the Promontory Hills.

The Formation of the Craigmont Orebody

Craigmont Orebody Two Hundred Million Years Old

Approximately 225 million years ago, a time known to geologists as the early Triassic Period, the Nicola Valley was covered with thousands of feet of volcanic rock. In places, including the slopes of the Promontory Hills, the waves of an ancient ocean lapped at the land. As millions of years passed, erosion deposited small fragments of broken rock and precipitated lime sediments on the ocean floor. In time, these sediments turned into rock as they were covered with other sediments and extensive lava flows from nearby volcanic action.

Guichon Batholith Formed

Near the end of the Triassic Period, about 198 million years ago, a molten body of rock from deep within the earth, now known as the Guichon Batholith, pushed its way into the early Triassic sedimentary and volcanic rocks. The massive forces from within the earth crushed, bent and folded the earth's crust as the vast volumes of molten rock moved upward.

The bed of limestone and the surrounding rock near the Promontory Hills were bent into the shape of a huge arch called an anticline. The rock that was once horizontal now stood almost vertical.

Guichon Batholith Provides Heat Source

As the Guichon Batholith slowly emerged from deep within the earth, stopping within five to 10 miles (eight to 16 kilometres) of the earth's surface, it created a source of intense heat that mobilized solutions within the surrounding rock. These reactive solutions dissolved some of the trace elements, including copper and iron. When these mobile solutions came in contact with the limestone from the ancient ocean beds, they reacted with the limestone to form copper and iron minerals. These concentrations, which became the Craigmont orebodies, are known as skarn deposits because of the mineral reaction to the limestone in the surrounding rock.

In contrast to the skarn deposits of the Craigmont orebody are the porphyry copper deposits of the Highland Valley, 18 miles (30 kilometres) to the north. As the batholith continued to form, the internal pressure built up and it caused the solidified rock near its center to crack and to fracture in millions of places. A copper-rich fluid escaped along these fractures. When this fluid cooled, it formed the porphyry copper deposits that are the source of copper for the Bethelehem, Lornex, Highmont and Valley Copper mines.

The creation of the Guichon Batholith was not an overnight happening, but rather an event that took millions of years. For about 80 million years following the upward movement of the earth's crust, trees grew on the ancient land surface while fast-flowing streams deeply cut into it.

About 100 million years ago during the Cretaceous Period, the eastern slopes of the Promontory Hills were suddenly covered with volcanic ash and molten lava. Like the recent activity on Mount St. Helens, the blast scattered the ancient forests and buried them with the volcanic debris. Clear evidence of the devastation was found in the form of petrified wood in the Craigmont open-pit mine.

After the volcanic action subsided, forests again flourished and erosion continued to remove material which covered the batholith. About 20 million years ago during the Miocene Period, lava flows again covered the region, but they were more extensive in the Kamloops area. Sediments deposited near Merritt at this time covered parts of the rich forests which were eventually turned to coal. The lava flows in the Nicola Valley and on the Promontory Hills were not thick and they were soon removed through erosion.

Glaciers Reshaped the Land

About one million years ago during what is known as the Pleistocene Period, glaciers covered almost all of Canada in a layer of ice as much as 3,000 feet (1,000 metres) thick. These glaciers ground into solid rock and reshaped the countryside which was left in much the same form as we know it today. The glacial action removed some of the lava covering the Craigmont orebodies, but it left a layer of gravel that partially filled the Nicola Valley and covered the slopes of the Promontory Hills. Seven feet (two metres) of gravel covered the highest outcropping of the orebody and hid it from the view of any prospector.

Orebody Relatively Small

There were no outcroppings on the surface to sample, but the wandering needle of Harry Merrell's compass suggested there was something beneath the surface. Ron Renshaw and Franklin Price explored these suspicions and, as diamond drillers, geologists and engineers followed, they created a three-dimensional map of the rock beneath the pine-covered slopes of the Promontory Hills.

Schematic section.

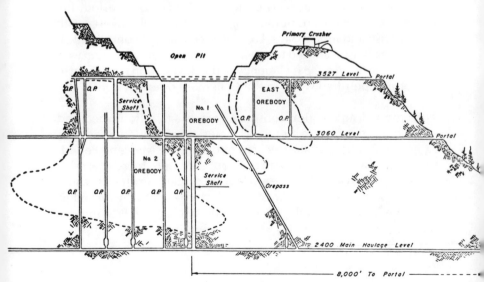

20

Through the use of technology, Renshaw and Price showed a chalcopyrite magnetite-specularite orebody, which had a combined strike length of about 2,805 feet (850 metres) and which extended over a vertical distance of 2,013 feet (610 metres), sat under their feet. The orebodies lay in steeply south-dipping Triassic Nicola Group rocks which paralleled the east-west contact of the south end of the Jurassic Guichon Batholith. None of the orebodies were exposed at the surface, but they were covered with a thin layer of glacial till or Cretaceous Kingsvale volcanic rocks.

Early Mining in the Nicola Valley

Natives were the First "Miners" in Nicola Valley

The Native people were British Columbia's first miners. Their stone-age culture used the rocks and the minerals to make tools and weapons. Products of volcanic action, such as obsidian and flint, were used to make sharp cutting edges. Natural copper was shaped and used for items of jewelry and trade.

When the last glaciation period ended some 10,000 years ago, Native Indians followed the retreating glaciers into what is now British Columbia. The first Indians to settle in the Nicola Valley were a small tribe of Athabaskans who travelled south from the Northwest Territories. Interior Salish Indians later came into the valley from the south via the Thompson and the Okanagan valleys and absorbed the Athabaskans into their culture.

Fur Traders Provided the First White Contact

Alexander Ross, a fur trader with the Pacific Fur Company, made the first known white contact with the Natives of the Nicola Valley in January, 1812. The Pacific Fur Company, North West Company and Hudson Bay Company successively maintained trading posts at Kamloops, but there was little activity in the Nicola Valley until 1846.

After the Boundary Treaty of 1846 effectively closed off the United States border to the traders, the Nicola Valley became part of the Fur Brigade route from the British Columbia Interior to Fort Hope on the Fraser River. Fur Brigades, which sometimes numbered as many as 400 horses and 50 men, carried their heavy loads of furs and trade goods through the grasslands of the valley and over the North

22

Cascade Mountains on a regular basis from 1848 until 1860.

Gold Prompts a Rush to British Columbia

The quiet lives of the fur trader and the Indian ended with the discovery of placer gold in the gravel bars of the Thompson and the Fraser rivers. As early as 1833, the traders reported traces of gold along the Pacific Coast and on the shores of Okanagan Lake. However, gold in quantities worth mining was not discovered until the early 1850s.

The Hudson's Bay Company kept the gold discovery quiet for several years, but when reports finally reached San Francisco in 1857, the rush began. By the autumn of 1858, 20,000 gold seekers were on their way to the Thompson and the Fraser rivers in search of the elusive yellow metal.

Nicola Coal Attracts Cattle Drovers

As the gold miners stampeded northward into the Cariboo, the Nicola Valley became an important, though sporadic, route of commerce. Cattle drovers, who brought their herds from as far south as Mexico, passed through the valley on their way to feed the hungry miners. One of these travellers discovered coal in the Nicola Valley, near where Merritt stands today, and carried some along with him for use in the blacksmith's shops along the Cariboo Wagon Road.

As the gold rush faltered, many miners left their pans and their sluice boxes behind in the Cariboo and headed south in search of land to farm. The mild climate and the open grasslands of the Nicola Valley attracted a number of the returning miners in the 1860s and the 1870s.

C.P.R. Spur-Line Helps
Old King Coal

After more than a decade of politics and false starts, a spur line of the Canadian Pacific Railway was constructed from the main line at Spences Bridge to the foot of Nicola Lake. The arrival of the first train in 1907 heralded the start of a mining era in the Nicola Valley. The coal that had been discovered beneath the nearby hills nearly four decades earlier had not been forgotten. Now the steam railway provided both a market and a means to move the coal to other markets.

The community of Merritt was established near the mines and it quickly grew to become a city April 1, 1911. When the Kettle Valley Railway was completed in 1916, Merritt became a boom town with three operating coal mines.

Coal Gives Way to Oil

As the demand for coal decreased with the introduction of oil-burning railway locomotives, Merritt's economy shifted from the mines to the abundant pine and Douglas fir forests that surrounded the grasslands. The depression of the 1930s saw the lumber market dwindle and with it went the hopes of the little community.

In a desperate move to save its primary industry, the city backed a loan to one of the sawmills; however, when the sawmill went bankrupt, the city went into receivership. Merritt grew with coal, switched to timber and now only the surrounding cattle ranches kept the city from becoming a ghost town.

Coal not the only Mineral
in the Nicola Valley

Coal was not the only mineral discovered in the Nicola Valley. Early miners heading for the Cariboo gold fields had discovered traces of gold in some of the creeks. However, credit for the most important geological work in the region must go to George M. Dawson of the Geological Survey of Canada for the detailed studies he started in 1877. Other geologists followed Dawson and they discovered traces of copper, iron, lead, zinc, silver and gold.

Some of these prospects became mines hailed into production with great fanfare only to slip quietly into oblivion when the ore ran out or the market conditions made the mines uneconomical.

Aberdeen Mine first on Promontory Hills

One of the early mining operations was the Aberdeen Mine, located west of Merritt, a short distance north of the present Craigmont site. According to reports, the first mineral showings at this location were discovered about 1897. Early development was limited as only small shipments of copper were made before the mine was abandoned. The Aberdeen Mine lay idle until 1916 when it was again reactivated. This time the mine shipped more than 1,400 tons (1,261 tonnes) of seven-per-cent copper ore before it again ceased operation.

There was some activity on the Aberdeen property in 1925, but it was not until 1928 that the mine reopened. Despite problems of flooding, the mine is reported to have produced nine ounces (280 grams) of gold, 761 ounces (24 kilograms) of silver and over 390,000 pounds (177,000 kilograms) of copper before it again closed.

"I reopened the Aberdeen Mine in the early 1960s for Torwest Resources Ltd., and shipped about 67 tons (60 tonnes) of 12-per-cent copper," said Ron Renshaw. "Water problems were excessive and the workings were allowed to flood."

Stumbles Discovers Copper-Iron Showing

While mining activity took place at several locations around the Nicola Valley in the 1930s, H. Stumbles trenched and diamond-drilled the Eric claim which was less than 1.2 miles (two kilometres) east of the present Craigmont open-pit mine. Although Stumbles did not discover a significant orebody, he did uncover copper and iron mineralization in the form of chalcopyrite and magnetite. Despite these showings, the next two decades saw little mining activity on the slopes of the Promontory Hills.

25

The Search for Financing

Neil McDiarmid
Promotes Craigmont

Despite the fact the diamond drilling program of 1957 showed the presence of a significant mineral deposit, Craigmont still did not have a mine. It would take millions of dollars and years of exploration, engineering and construction before the orebody would provide a return to the investors.

Neil H. McDiarmid had a vision unblunted with harsh realities. McDiarmid thought he had a billion-ton mine. He visualized a copper smelter, an iron smelter and a steel industry based on the copper and the iron in the Promontory Hills and the coal near Merritt.

"My husband wanted to keep our natural resources in Canada, not sell everything to Japan," said Lucile McDiarmid.

"McDiarmid was the original promoter," said John Simpson, then president of Placer Development, "but do not speak harshly of promoters because promoters have done a great job for Canada."

"Promoters give the most optimistic side of the story and that rakes in the cash to get the mine going. You cannot have a pessimist going out and saying, 'This mine is not much good, how about putting in a thousand dollars.'"

McDiarmid's optimism infected a number of small investors. Richard Ricardo of the Railway Club is said to have put in the first $1,000. Senator Stan McKeen, Anthony Arnold, Earl Olts, Whitey Wilson, Raymond Collishaw and many others contributed cash, know-how and prestige to the project. However, now Craigmont needed big money — millions of dollars — before the copper-iron deposit could become a mine.

26

Placer Development Approached

It is difficult to determine how many people or how many companies McDiarmid approached with his dream of a giant copper mine. According to John Simpson, E.P. (Ted) Chapman, Jr. of Chapman, Wood and Griswold, suggested their client, Vernon Taylor, take an interest in Craigmont. Ted Chapman was a geologist and his firm acted as a consultant to both Craigmont and to Taylor's Peerless Oil and Gas Company. Taylor telephoned John Simpson of Placer and he suggested the prospect might be one more suited for Placer's area of expertise. After Placer's geologists and engineers studied the diamond-drill core samples and the drilling results, they gave the prospect a favorable report.

The American Smelting and Refining Company had an option on the Craigmont property at the time and when they let it drop, Placer's subsidiary, Canadian Explorations Ltd., purchased shares in Craigmont which provided the much-needed funding for continued assessment of the orebody. By this time, Noranda Mines Ltd. had acquired claims near the Craigmont orebody and had also purchased shares in Craigmont. With the interest and the financial backing of Placer, Noranda and Peerless Oil and Gas — three recognized mining companies — Craigmont's future looked bright.

Placer Development Invests

Placer Had a Golden Start

Placer Development Ltd. was formed in 1926 as the result of a visit to Vancouver from miner-turned-lawyer William A. Freeman. Freeman stopped off in Vancouver during a visit to Seattle where he was to line up the Australian rights to the manufacture and the distribution of Jantzsen swim suits. Before he left Australia, friends told him to look in on Charles Arthur Banks, a New Zealand-born mining engineer who lived in British Columbia. Their meeting led to the formation of Placer Development Ltd., a company which had offices in Vancouver and San Francisco.

Gold Dredges in New Guinea

One of Placer's first major mining projects began in 1928 with a gold-dredging operation in the tropical mountains of New Guinea. Dredges, made in small units for on-site assembly, were flown in with Junkers aircraft for a new subsidiary, Bulolo Gold Dredging Ltd. Bulolo was Placer's first big success as it made $1.5 million in net profits during 1935, a time when the world economy was at a low ebb. The Bulolo workings produced $75 million in gold before they were closed in 1961. From Bulolo, Placer advanced into another successful gold venture on the Nechi River in Colombia.

Placer also became involved in oil in Texas and California for a decade before it sold out; Placer turned an original investment of $900,000 into $13 million at the time of sale. While it was in the oil business Placer set a record of sorts as it put down 26 test holes in Texas without hitting a single dry hole — 17 holes produced high-grade oil.

Placer's first venture in Canada came in 1947 with the acquisition of the Emerald underground tungsten mine near Salmo, B.C. which also had extensive deposits of lead and zinc. This shift from placer mining to underground mining helped to create a new area of expertise in the Placer group of companies and it set the stage for a

Placer subsidiary, Canadian Exploration Ltd. (Canex), to expand its interests.

Placer Invests Money and Expertise in Craigmont

In November, 1957, Canadian Exploration Ltd., a Placer subsidiary, injected new financial and technical resources into Craigmont as it took charge of the exploration program. Work continued through the winter. Hole 15 warmed the cold February weather when it intersected 660 feet (201 metres) of ore which averaged 4.35 per cent copper. Craigmont was now no longer just a prospect, it was on its way to becoming a copper mine.

Preparing for Production

Birkett Creek Mine Operators Formed

On June 1, 1958, Canex joined forces with Noranda and Peerless Oil to form Birkett Creek Mine Operators Ltd. as the operating company. This new company signed an agreement with Craigmont to proceed with exploration and development. The necessary plant installation to bring the mine into production would follow later.

Exploration work continued on the surface while tunnels (adits) were driven into the mountain to determine the size and the nature of the orebody and to extract large amounts of ore for further study. Based on these studies, the company made the decision to begin mining through the open-pit method and it planned to change to an underground operation when the pit reached its maximum safe depth.

By early 1960, the company had outlined three separate orebodies with an estimated 22,575,000 tons (20,337,837 tonnes) of ore which averaged 2.08 per cent copper and 19.6 per cent iron. Work was well underway on a 4,000 tons-per-day (3,604 tonnes-per-day) concentrator at the 2,400-foot (727 metres) level.

After careful consideration, Birkett Creek Mine Operators Ltd. was phased out January 1, 1960. Strong financial incentives, coupled with the fact Neil H. McDiarmid's efforts had made the Craigmont name well known in mining circles, influenced the decision. The major shareholders maintained their respective interests in Craigmont while Canex (Placer) supervised the operation.

Preparing pit for production Aug. 1961.
George Allen Aerial Photos Ltd.

Production Preparation a Mammoth Job

Before open-pit mining could begin, hundreds of feet of waste and overburden had to be removed from the orebody. Peter Kiewit Sons of Canada Ltd. began the mammoth removal task in June, 1960; by March, 1961, the company had cleared away 3,555,000 cubic yards (2,718,007 cubic metres) of rock and glacial till. Craigmont personnel then began the first phase of preparing for the mining operation.

Clay Created Problems

Clay, left behind from the glacial lakes that once inundated the Nicola Valley, created construction problems. Andre Orbeliani, a design engineer who came to Craigmont from the Jersey Mine at Salmo, B.C., had the task of dealing with the uncertain ground.

"Clay is a solid base as long as it is dry," recalled Andre Orbeliani, "but it becomes a great problem if disturbed and wetted. Wet clay will yield under pressure and flow and no building is safe if the clay becomes wet."

Craigmont's engineers not only faced layers of clay at the mill site, they also faced layers of clay at a nearby creek that supplied water to lubricate the clay.

Special care had to be taken with the foundations of the mill and the fine ore bins because of the weight they would carry when the system went into service.

"In spite of all precautions," recalled Andre, "the foundations of the big machines, the rod and the ball mills moved under the load and these foundations had to be extended after operations commenced."

Craigmont Largest Load on B. C. Hydro System

"The construction of a 60,000-volt transmission line from Merritt to Craigmont, 10.5 miles (17.5 kilometres) northwest of Merritt is nearing completion. . ." said a story in the *Merritt Herald*. "Craigmont Mines has a power contract with B. C. Hydro for 5,000 kilowatts, the largest industrial load on B. C. Hydro's mainland system."

Preproduction Costs Total $18 Million

By September, 1961, Craigmont officials were ready to throw the switch that would start the process of turning raw ore into copper concentrate for shipment to smelters in Japan and in the United States. It had been almost four years since hole seven sparked Placer's interest in Craigmont. Exploration and development to the production stage had required over one million man-hours with a payroll of $2.5 million. Contractors required more than 800,000 man-hours with a payroll of $2 million. The total cost of exploration and development was approximately $18 million before the mine began earning any income.

The city of Merritt had also experienced the biggest boom in its 50-year history. In the last year of activity, the quiet ranching and logging village of 1,500 people had become a bustling mining community of more than double that population.

Craigmont design engineer Andre Orbeliani.   **Craigmont photo**

Volume 1, Number 1 of the new *"The Pacific Miner"* tabloid hailed the official opening of Craigmont as a "Triumph of Modern Engineering."

Craigmont official opening.

Craigmont photo

Craigmont Mine and Mill in Production

New British Columbia Copper Giant Holds Opening Ceremony.

"On Friday, September 15, (1961) some 350 government, mining, business and civic leaders gathered at Craigmont Mines to mark the official opening of this tremendous addition to the ranks of British Columbia's metal producers."

Official Opening (L-R): Neil McDiarmid, Ross Duthie, Betty Duthie, Allan Collett.   **Craigmont photo**

"Formal opening was performed by British Columbia's Mines Minister W.K. Kiernan, attended by Craigmont's President J.D. Simpson, Vice-President and General Manager G.A. Gordon, Mine Superintendent Ross Duthie and pioneer directors Neil McDiarmid and Earl Olts."

Even R.M. Shaw, business editor of the Vancouver *"Province"*, waxed eloquent in his description of the opening in the September 18, 1961 issue of the paper:

"In brilliant sunshine last Friday afternoon, 350 people stood on a ledge up at the 4,200-foot (1,273-metre) level on Promontory Mountain.

"Immediately below their feet was a huge 'open cut' mining operation."

"Twenty-seven ton (24 tonne) 'Eucs' — Euclid dump trucks — whipped about like jeeps, their powerful diesels growling like angry lions. Shovels lifting four and a half tons at a bite loaded the trucks with copper ore from the benches."

Canada's respected mining publication, *"The Northern Miner,"* stated Craigmont was "destined to become one of Canada's great mines and a major copper producer."

W.K. (Ken) Kiernan officially starts the Craigmont operation September 15, 1961. (l-r) Kiernan, G. Gordon, John Simpson.

Craigmont photo

Giant Open-pit Mine

Mining the Craigmont orebody was no simple task. The company pioneered open-pit mining in Western Canada. Giant drills prepared the holes for explosives. Three 4.5-cubic-yard (3.4-cubic-metre) electric shovels loaded the broken ore into fourteen 27-cubic-yard (21-cubic-metre) Euclid diesel trucks for transportation to the gyrator crusher located at the 3,700-foot (1,128-metre) elevation on the rim of the pit.

"It was, I believe, a well laid out, efficiently run open-pit operation," says Ross Duthie. "(It was) probably as good as any operation in the world."

Cable Belt Conveyor Carried Ore More Than A Mile

Craigmont's engineers faced a formidable task in attempting to devise a method of moving thousands of tons of ore per day down the mountain slope. Truck haulage was eliminated because of the long, steep grade to the 2,400-foot (727-metre) level mill site. Elevator or skip haulage and underground orepasses were eliminated because of cost, construction time and winter freezing problems. The engineers finally decided on a cable-supported belt system with an overall length of 5,710 feet (1,740 metres) and a fall of 1,121 feet (342 metres). The belt was 30 inches (76 centimetres) wide

36

and it rested on special 1.5-inch (four-centimetre) diameter steel cables that supported and drove the belt. The cables were in turn driven with a 370-horsepower electric motor and the belt was capable of carrying 400 tons (360 tonnes) of ore per hour. The electric motor was only needed to start the conveyor belt or to run it while it was empty. Under a normal load, the motor acted as a generator and served as a brake. Thus, the electricity generated was fed in to the gyratory crusher system which reduced the demand from B.C. Hydro. The conveyor system cost $400,000, a significant expenditure at that time.

Cable conveyor belt ready for operation August, 1961.
George Allen Aerial Photos Ltd.

The belt conveyor system dumped the crushed ore into a stockpile which fed secondary and tertiary cone crushers. After crushing, the ore was stored in a 8,500-ton (7,658-tonne) capacity fine-ore bin.

Blast hole drill at Craigmont open-pit mine.

Concentrator Removed Waste Rock

In the final stage of the concentrating process, the ore was ground to the fineness of talcum powder with two rod mills and two ball mills in parallel. In this form, a differential flotation system separated the finely-ground copper mineral of chalcopyrite from the waste particles. After thickening to remove and to recycle excess water, the waste rock was piped to a tailing holding pond. After filtering to remove excess water, the concentrate was ready to be trucked to the railway siding at Coyle, British Columbia, a distance of about five miles (eight kilometres) for shipment to the smelters.

Japanese and American Contracts Signed

Even before construction of the mine and the 4,000-tons-per-day (3,603-tonnes-per-day) concentrator were started, Craigmont had negotiated firm sales contracts for its copper concentrate. The major portion of the copper concentrate was sold to Japanese smelters, including Sumitomo Metal Mining Company, Nippon Mining Company and Mitsubishi Metal Mining Company, as part of a six-year contract. The American Smelting and Refining Company at Tacoma, Washington, agreed to take a portion of the concentrate.

The first shipload, which amounted to 7,355 tons (6,129 long wet tons) of chalcopyrite concentrate which averaged 28.7 per cent copper, left Vancouver for Japan November 8, 1961. Shipments to AS and R's Tacoma smelter began early in 1962. (Note: A long wet ton is the equivalent of a metric tonne or 2,200 lbs.)

Craigmont's management had also negotiated a four-year labor agreement with Local 1011 of the International Union of Mine, Mill and Smelter Workers which was to expire in July, 1965. This agreement promised a period of labor stability for the company during the start-up or the "pay-back" period, the period during which the company would pay back its bank loans.

Battery operated locomotive hauls train out of Craigmont exploration drift. August, 1961.

George Allen Aerial Photos Ltd.

Conservative Engineering in Craigmont's Favor

Craigmont's engineers and geologists had been conservative in their estimates on at least two counts. In the case of the mill design, they over-estimated the difficulty in crushing and milling the ore. With only minimal modification, they were able to increase the capacity from 4,000 to 5,000 tons (3600 to 4500 tonnes) per day by mid-1962. In addition to this increase, the open-pit mine produced a richer grade of ore than originally anticipated.

Bank Loans Quickly Repaid

Craigmont's annual report for the year which ended October 31, 1962, the first full year of operation, reflected a "gratifying" picture of the company's financial state. With a net profit of $10,739,000, the company was able to begin paying off its bank loans and its preferred shareholders. By December, 1962, all the bank borrowings of $7,560,000 (U.S.) had been repaid. All of the preferred shares were redeemed before the end of 1964 at a cost of almost $8 million. Government regulations allowed Craigmont a tax-free period of three years which ended September 30, 1964, but with tax allowances for preproduction and capital costs, the company did not have to pay taxes until March, 1967.

Thomas Canino — Laborer, Craigmont was "home" for 21 years. (December, 1982). **Murphy Shewchuk photo**

Underground Mining

Underground Exploration Begun in 1958

Surface development and preparation for open-pit mining began in 1958. Craigmont began operating as an open-pit mine in August, 1961, when the first ore was put through the mill, and continued as an open-pit operation until March, 1967. Underground exploration and development work began in July, 1958, first to establish the size and the nature of the orebody and second to determine the best method of underground mining. When the open-pit operation ceased, underground mining gradually increased until it provided all of the ore for the milling operation.

The early work indicated the ore was separated into three distinct pockets or orebodies and the rock had a fractured and unstable quality which required caution during mining.

Tony Petrina started with the operating group, Birkett Creek Mine Operators Ltd., as a mining engineer in November, 1960. Petrina was assigned the long-term task of developing a satisfactory method of mining when the open pit could no longer be used.

The sublevel caving method of mining, a method developed in Sweden and, at the time, untried in North America, was initially considered and rejected because the "dilution rate" was too high. "We would have had to take out too much waste to get the ore," said Petrina.

Conventional Mining Methods Rejected

"We tried two conventional underground mining methods at Craigmont," said Petrina. "One of them was simple blasthole stoping which is a fairly common method, but we had to have very solid ground to do that. We did not have it at Craigmont. (This method), nevertheless, was profitable, but it was only applicable to

42

a small part of the orebody."

The "stope" in mining terminology is as important to the under-ground production area as the kitchen is important to the restaurant. A number of stopes are usually located within the ore zone so large quantities of the ore can be mined. In blasthole stoping, holes are drilled into the rock, filled with explosives and detonated. As a result, the rock is loosened so it can be removed. At Craigmont, the fractured nature of the orebody made such an operation difficult to control and, therefore, dangerous.

"The other method we tried on a larger scale was cut-and-fill stoping. That is quite an expensive mining method," said Petrina.

In cut-and-fill stoping, the ore is removed in seven to 10-foot (two to three-metre) thick slices or layers and the space created is filled with waste which often consists of the tailings from the mill.

"The problem with cut-and-fill was that we ended up with underground openings that were too large which we could not support safely," said Petrina. "I would say that the success with blasthole stoping was limited and cut-and-fill was not very profitable. The mine would have ended a lot sooner had we continued with either method."

Swedish Mining Method Adopted

In 1965, a group of Craigmont engineers, including Tony Petrina and Placer's Vice President, Operations, C. L. Pillar, visited Sweden to study the sublevel caving method of mining. They decided the method warranted much closer examination under the difficult rock conditions found at Craigmont.

"We built models and tried them," said Andre Orbeliani. "We made pictures and even films and finally we tried this method underground. It has been used extensively since that time in our mine and in other mines where conditions were similar."

As the period of open-pit mining at Craigmont drew to a close due to costs and the safe depth that could be reached, the decision was made to adopt the sublevel caving method of extracting the ore from the underground orebodies. This decision set in motion a series of events which placed Craigmont on the road to mining history in Canada.

Sublevel caving is best described as a retreat method of mining in which the orebody is mined in horizontal slices from the top to the bottom and from one side to the other. Essential for the method to work is to have loose waste rock cave in and continually envelope the ore when it is blasted loose for extraction. In Craigmont, the surrounding waste rock was also heavily fractured; thus, caving easily occurred and the waste rock was able to fill the void left after the valuable ore was removed.

Transverse sublevel caving.

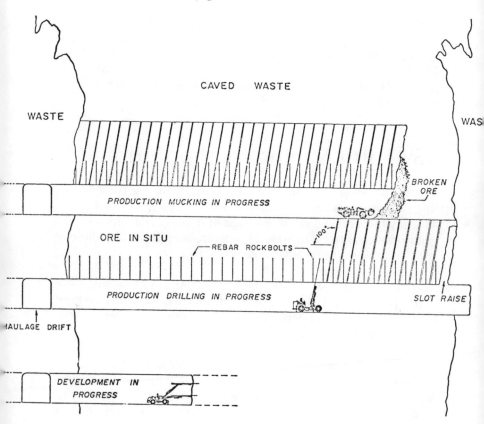

Pit Floor Covered by 40-Foot Layer of Waste

In the main orebody at Craigmont, the waste cover was initially provided by placing a 40-foot (12-metre) layer of waste rock over the entire floor of the open pit. As mining progressed downward, the walls of the pit caved to provide further cover.

Starting just below the floor of the open pit, sublevels were driven across the orebody at 31-foot (10-metre) intervals. Work was simultaneously carried out on three or more sublevels as the mining operations of drilling, blasting and mucking took place on the upper sublevels while development and ground support operations took place on the lower sublevels. The ore was broken by drilling fans of two-inch (five-centimetre) diameter upward-looking holes and blasting the fans one at a time. The ore was removed after each blast and it was dumped into vertical steel-lined orepasses from which it dropped to bins on the 2,400-foot level (732 metres above sea level).

At the 2,400-foot (732-metre) level, electric locomotives hauled the ore out to the mill and the crusher on the surface in 16-ton (14-tonne) capacity ore cars.

Miners Faced Difficulties

The sublevel caving method of mining was not without its difficulties. Problems were encountered with the blasting of the rings of holes, but the addition of special timbering techniques helped to prevent the unblasted holes from being broken or plugged.

The problem of dilution (caved waste mixed with ore) initially plagued the operation, but the problem was gradually corrected until it was reduced to about 30 per cent. Ore recovery also reached approximately 90 per cent by the early 1970s.

First in Canada

Craigmont's experience with large-scale sublevel caving was a first in Canada. As a result, Craigmont attracted considerable attention in the mining industry. The system was the subject of a paper presented in April, 1970, to the Canadian Institute of Mining and Metalurgy by A.J. (Tony) Petrina and his colleagues, D.L. Pillar and E.W. Cokayne. E.W. Cokayne also gave a talk on the subject to a Swedish group in August, 1972.

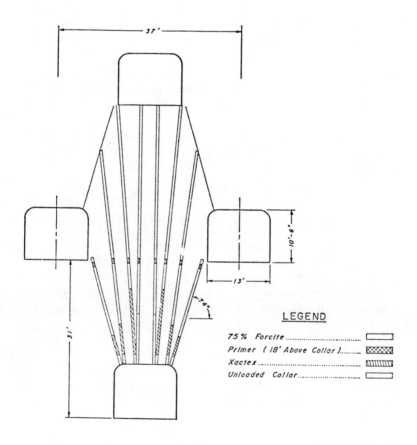

LEGEND

75 % Forcite	
Primer (18' Above Collar)	
Xactex	
Unloaded Collar	

Drilling patterns — sublevel caving.

46

Trackless Equipment Used

Prior to the mid-twentieth century, most underground mines used small compressed air mining equipment. Small steel-wheeled mine cars similar to railway cars provided transportation which moved men and equipment in the mines and brought out the ore. On the main haulage ways, trolley wires suspended from the tunnel ceiling powered electric locomotives. In the lesser-used tunnels or drifts, smaller electric locomotives carried large storage batteries which provided the power.

Craigmont used electric mine locomotives powered with trolley wires on the main haulage in the 2,400-foot (732-metre) level.

"One unique feature of the main electric haulage system was that the power was supplied in the lines as A.C. (alternating current)," said Ross Duthie, the mine manager from 1958 to 1964. "Up to this time, the standard was D.C. (direct current). The use of A.C. was made possible with the development of silicon rectifiers. N. J. Smortchevsky — Placer's electrical engineer — devised the system, supervised the manufacture of the rectifier units used in the locomotives and literally worked day and night to iron out the problems."

This method, pioneered at Craigmont, is now commonly used elsewhere. These powerful locomotives ran on steel rails or tracks and were capable of pulling up to 12 cars, each loaded with 256 cubic feet (seven cubic metres) or 16 tons (14 tonnes) of ore.

"We had the most modern locomotives available on our main haulage," said Andre Orbeliani. "We had an ore-car dumping mechanism that was unique and close to automatic. After the operator drove the ore train to the dump, he stood on an elevated platform and, by pushing buttons, he could dump the cars and move the train to a new position."

Pioneered at Salmo

The actual mining operation at Craigmont used equipment that was rubber-tired, self-propelled and operated without steel rails or tracks.

"It was another Placer company that pioneered the use of trackless mining equipment at the Jersey Mine at Salmo in the early 1950s," said Tony Petrina. "When Craigmont began operation in the mid-1960s, we used the second generation of such equipment."

Modifications Needed

The use of this equipment required innovation and imagination on the part of Craigmont's engineers and tradesmen.

In 1970, the Number One East orebody required special attention because of its small size and because it was cut off from the main orebody. To deal with these problems, Craigmont's engineers purchased Swedish-made Cavo air-powered load-haul-dump mining equipment and modified it to suit their needs. In this instance, they "married" two different-sized autoloaders and operated one through remote control, a feat considered new in North America at the time.

"The Scooptram trackless mining equipment we used in the main orebody was not in wide use elsewhere in the mining industry," added Petrina. "It was diesel powered with special scrubbers to remove carbon monoxide and nitrous oxides from the exhaust. The Scooptram equipment was a combination loader and hauler. It was called load-haul-dump (LHD) because it did everything with one machine. The Scooptram could pick up five cubic yards (four cubic metres) of ore, about eight or nine tons (seven to eight tonnes), and transport it to the orepasses."

The use of diesel-powered equipment also required better ventilation than was common in mines of the period. Craigmont's engineers used computers to assist in the design of the air circulation; the result was a marked increase in productivity.

Logging Equipment Modified

An important part of the mining operation involved drilling a fan of holes in the orebody in which to place explosives so the ore could be blasted loose. Unlike the days of drill steel and sledge hammers, drilling had become a highly-mechanized operation as machines drove several drills at a time.

In 1972, the need for increased mobility of this equipment, in order to meet production goals, necessitated converting one of Craigmont's existing drills to a diesel-driven machine.

To achieve the needed mobility, the engineers looked outside the mining industry and purchased a John Deere model 440 logging skidder. The articulating chassis of this machine was modified to accept the drilling booms and the associated equipment from an existing Gardner Denver fan drill. A Deutz four-cylinder diesel engine fitted to the skidder's robust transmission provided the mobility.

The crossbred equipment worked so well the skidder chassis was used for more fan drills, jumbo drills and a variety of custom-built underground service vehicles.

Electric locomotive used on Craigmont 2400 level main haulage.
Craigmont photo

The underground roads had to be maintained and kept free of mud and water for efficient operation, but the limited space made conventional equipment difficult, if not impossible, to use. At one stage of the operation, Craigmont purchased a Galion model 503A grader for use underground. Before it was put into service, the shop tradesmen modified it, installed a front bumper, reinforced the frame and lowered the operator's platform, seat and steering controls eight inches (20 centimetres) to decrease overall height.

The motto of the mechanical department was, said Andre Orbeliani, "GIVE US THE VERY BEST EQUIPMENT AND WE WILL IMPROVE IT."

Shotcrete Used to Support Tunnel Walls

"Another unusual feature of Craigmont was our method of ground support by spraying concrete on the walls," said Tony Petrina. "I do not think anybody had done that before to the extent we did it."

The fractured quality of the rock was one reason Craigmont used sprayed concrete (shotcrete) instead of timbers to support the underground work zones and passageways. The second reason was the space needed to maneuver the trackless mining equipment.

"There was also a risk the mining equipment might knock out support timbers and cause a cave-in," added Tony Petrina. "We decided if we could get rid of the timber, we could reduce the hazard and make the tunnels a little bit smaller."

"Depending on how fractured the rock was, we would tunnel anywhere from 10 to 100 feet (three to 30 metres) before having to set up the equipment to spray concrete on the walls. The concrete was about two inches (five centimetres) thick and when it hardened, it formed an eggshell-like structure that held the rock in place and kept the air away from it."

The shotcreting operation was highly mechanized. A two-man crew using a truck to haul sand and cement and a combination compressed air mixer and sprayer mounted on a modified skidder could spray 17 to 33 feet (five to 10 metres) of tunnel during an eight-hour shift.

Orepasses an Engineering Feat

In most underground mines, the rock is solid enough that orepasses (vertical openings in the rock through which the broken ore is dropped to collection bins) can be used without special linings. However, at Craigmont the rock was so badly fractured that raw orepasses soon wore away and collapsed. Therefore, the orepasses had to be reinforced and designed so the falling ore would not compact into a solid mass at the bottom.

Orepasses Critical

"The location of the orepasses was critical," said Tony Petrina. "They were steel and concrete lined and they cost millions of dollars to build. The Scooptram machines were good loading units, but they were not very efficient hauling units so we had to balance the cost of hauling the ore with the cost of building the orepasses. The average haul distance was approximately 750 feet (230 metres) and the maximum haul distance was approximately 2,000 feet (610 metres)."

Steel and Concrete Lined Orepasses

To construct the orepasses, Craigmont hired a contractor with boring equipment to drill eight-foot (2.4-metre) diameter holes between the working levels in the mine. These holes were lined with steel plates which were backed with concrete for support. The orepasses were offset at fixed intervals and they were built with rock boxes to slow the falling rock at each level.

The construction of the orepasses was time consuming and expensive. One set of orepasses, constructed in the summer of 1971, required over 150 tons (135 tonnes) of steel and 450 yards (344 cubic metres) of concrete. The construction of the "780" orepass, with a total vertical drop of 500 feet (152 metres) and a 1,000-ton (901-tonne) ore bin at the 2,400-foot (732-metre) level, took six months.

Utilizing the Magnetite

Iron Smelters Visualized

Neil H. McDiarmid had great hopes for a steel industry based on Craigmont's iron content in the copper ore and Nicola Valley coal. "He was a wild optimist," said John Simpson. "He visualized iron smelters here and a smelter for copper. He thought he had a billion-ton mine."

The company conducted studies on ways to recover the magnetite and hematite from the milling operation. "While it is clear that recovery of iron at Craigmont is technically feasible," stated the 1962 annual report, "it is increasingly evident that suitable freight rates and product prices will be essential if such an operation is to be profitable."

A practical market could not be found for the magnetite and hematite that were part of the Craigmont orebody. During the initial years of operation, the iron ore was relegated to the tailing pond.

Iron Used to Clean Coal

In 1968, Kaiser Coal (now British Columbia Resources) signed a long-term contract with Japanese steel producers to supply coking coal at the rate of three million tons (2,702 tonnes) per year. Additional contracts brought this total up to five million tons (4,504 tonnes) per year.

Kaiser was required to supply high-quality coking coal; this area is where Craigmont entered the picture. One phase of the upgrading of raw coal involves passing it through a heavy media or sink float plant. The specific gravity of the media is maintained at a level which allows the coal to float off and the gangue or the waste material to sink to the bottom. The coal is further processed to remove the dust and to recover the attached heavy media.

Craigmont "Waste" Becomes a Valuable Commodity

The heavy media selected for the process was magnetite, a heavy media of which Craigmont had plentiful supplies. A contract was signed for the purchase of a minimum of 5,000 tons (4500 tonnes) per year. Kaiser's specifications were rigid as the company required high-grade magnetite finer than 325 mesh — particles smaller than 0.003 inches (0.08 millimetres) in diameter. After considerable research, the plant modifications were made at a cost of $164,000. The new concentrator circuit was capable of recovering up to 75 tons (68 tonnes) of magnetite per day from the mill tailings. Rail shipments of magnetite began in December, 1969. By October 31, 1970, Craigmont had produced 17,331 tons (15,614 tonnes) of high-grade magnetite concentrate for shipment to coal producers in British Columbia and Alberta. In 1971, the recovery circuit was enlarged to a capacity of 50,000 tons (45,000 tonnes) per year.

Craigmont Becomes Major Supplier

By the end of 1972, Craigmont had become the principal source of fine magnetite in western Canada. Sales revenue for this product had reached $641,000, double the 1971 figure.

Over the next decade, magnetite became an increasingly important part of Craigmont's output. In 1981, half of the milling system was reorganized to reprocess the coarse magnetite that had been previously stockpiled. In March, 1982, with the completion of the copper ore processing, the milling system was completely converted to processing magnetite.

McDiarmid's dream of an iron smelter was no closer to reality. Instead, in an almost ironical twist of fate, Craigmont's iron was helping to clean British Columbia coal bound for Japanese smelters.

Ending Underground Operation

The Day the Mine Runs Dry

Mining deals with a finite or limited resource. Factors other than just the size of the orebody govern the life of a mine. Employment depends on the mineral market as well as the ore that lies in the ground.

"It was obvious from the outset that the Merritt mine could not last more than 18 years," said Placer's W. D. Thompson in a 1978 *"Financial Times"* story. "So in 1971, the company and its employees started planning for the last day."

Life Extended at Craigmont

The Craigmont mine received two reprieves from its impending early 1979 closure. The rise in copper prices during late 1978, in combination with the premium on U.S. currency, effectively lowered the cutoff grade of ore mined to 0.7 per cent from one per cent. To add to the reserves, Craigmont employees discovered the underground waste dump assayed at 0.38 per cent copper. Despite the low grade, it was economical to process the "waste" because it helped to keep the mill operating at its optimum level.

Craigmont was again expected to close in mid-1981 due to depletion of its ore reserves, but under a milling procedure introduced early in 1981 that involved dividing the system into two parts — one half for copper and one half for regrinding stockpiled magnetite — the life of the operation was extended to the end of 1982. Mining continued into early 1982 and, when the last of the copper ore was processed in March, the milling operation was completely converted to process the magnetite.

Ray Archer in "Dry" at Craigmont.

Murphy Shewchuk Photo

Severance Programs Initiated

Two severance programs were initiated to assist those employees who stayed to the end of operations in order to bridge the period between jobs. The employees and the company jointly funded a savings plan as each contributed five cents per hour worked while Craigmont solely funded the completion bonus plan. With each contract renewal, the completion bonus was sweetened as it reached $1.00 per hour at the end.

On the average, both programs paid out approximately $8,000 per employee when their employment was terminated.

Mike Witham on last ore train out of mine.

Vancouver Sun photo

Grinding operator Thomas Roth — shutting down after 21 years of operation. (December, 1982)

Murphy Shewchuk photo

Ore Reserve Estimates "Dead-On"

Initial estimates of Craigmont's ore reserves, based on exploration drilling to the end of 1960, were 22,575,000 tons which averaged 2.08 per cent copper. This percentage works out to 939 million pounds or 426 kilograms of copper.

When production was completed in 1982, the company had mined 36,750,000 tons of ore which averaged 1.28 per cent copper. The difference in the percentage of copper was primarily due to mining methods that resulted in the extraction of a greater amount of waste rock than originally planned. The amount of copper actually produced was almost exactly equal to the original estimates.

A Canadian Press story, datelined Merritt, December 19, 1981, heralded the final stage of Craigmont's mining operation:

Old Hand Drills Craigmont's Last Hole

"Miner John Roberts, 56, started drilling the first drift at Craigmont Mines Ltd. near this southern Interior community in 1958."

"Last week he drilled the final round of holes in the last drift to be driven in the mine."

"The copper producer has depleted its ore reserves and will cease all mining operations at the end of January."

"After all the remaining ore has been removed . . . underground equipment will be brought to the surface and all mine entrances will be sealed."

"Roberts is not bitter about the impending end to his 23-year association with Craigmont."

" 'There is nothing left to mine, so there is not much they can do,' " he shouted over the roar of his three-boom drill jumbo in the drift at the 2,606-foot (796-metre) sublevel.

" 'It has been a good run here and I have enjoyed it. I would not have stayed around this long if I had not.' "

The last ore train rolled out the 2,400-foot (732-metre) February 15, 1982, with Mike Witham at the controls. Mining at Craigmont was completed and all that remained of the copper operation was to process the 40,000 tons (36,000 tonnes) of ore on the surface stockpile. The task of removing the equipment from the underground operation and sealing the mine entrances could now be completed.

John Roberts drills last hole at Craigmont in December, 1981.
Kamloops Daily photo

Outside Exploration

Mine Site Explored

From its early beginnings, Craigmont was involved with local exploration to determine if there were any other ore deposits adjacent to the mine.

An active surface exploration program which employed geochemical and geophysical methods was carried out on Craigmont property during the summer of 1966. Underground diamond drilling outlined more ore in the known orebodies. Several other properties in the Merritt area were examined at the same time.

In 1976, an on-site exploration program was conducted in a last-ditch attempt to find a new orebody adjacent to Craigmont.

In May, 1978, Craigmont manager Bill Diment stated the company's $1.6 million exploration program had been unsuccessful.

"It was unsuccessful," said Diment, "but I do not think I have to worry about somebody else finding an orebody under my nose for the forseeable future."

On-site exploration of a fashion did help prolong the life of the mining operation when an additional 700,000 tons (630,630 tonnes) of low-grade ore was "discovered" through the drilling of the open-pit waste dumps.

"The waste dumps singled out for attention were the earlier ones where the 'cut-off grade' was purposely held high to expedite the repayment of the development costs," said Diment.

Douglas Lake Ranch

In 1968, Craigmont examined 13 mining properties in the area. Exploration, including some diamond drilling work, continued on the Douglas Plateau in 1969 and 1970, but when no viable ore deposits were found, the program was discontinued.

Kamad Silver

In 1970, Craigmont reached an agreement with Kamad Silver Mines Ltd., for exploration work on their property near Adams Lake, but again the search did not uncover an orebody considered economical.

Unimog #5 — Outside Craigmont shops March, 1969.

Craigmont photo

Hank Happner — Assay Lab, Craigmont. (December, 1982)
Murphy Shewchuk photo

Exploration Division Formed

In the spring of 1972, Craigmont started an exploration division, based in Kamloops, for the purpose of exploring for economic mineral deposits in the south-central part of British Columbia. Nels Vollo, previously employed with Royal Canadian Ventures, was installed as exploration manager with an annual budget of approximately $200,000. This amount varied throughout the decade as it reached as much as $1 million.

Nels Vollo and his field man, Leo Loranger, were Craigmont's total exploration staff throughout most of the following decade. Their assignment was to purchase, to option or to discover an economic orebody that could become the next "home" for Craigmont's staff and equipment.

With the aid of various contracting drillers, geologists and aerial exploration firms, Vollo and Loranger carried out an intensive grass-roots exploration program in the regions north and east of Kamloops, British Columbia. They finished about 36,300 feet (11,000 metres) of exploration diamond drilling on a massive sulphide deposit near Chu-Chua in the Barriere area. The deposit contained copper and significant amounts of gold and silver, but it was not considered large enough to return the capital costs of starting a mine.

Craigmont also explored other properties throughout the province. The Redbird molybdenum property near Smithers, British Columbia, looked encouraging until the bottom dropped out of the molybdenum market. The Iron Mask copper and gold property near Kamloops also looked promising until metal prices plummetted during the depression of the 1980s.

Despite considerable effort, Craigmont was unable to come up with a viable orebody before the end of 1982.

"We came pretty close in a few instances," says Vollo. "But we did not quite make it. The Redbird property and the Iron Mask property will eventually be mined, but not at today's prices."

Reclamation

Stearman Biplane Roared over Craigmont

The roar of a World War Two Stearman biplane echoed across the valley and bounced off the walls of the Craigmont open pit.

Although the casual observer may have questioned his senses, it was not a case where the clock had been turned back; instead, it was the beginning of a program to turn back the clock. The date was October, 1969, and the biplane had been converted to carry a payload of 1,800 pounds (820 kilograms) of fertilizer or 1,000 pounds (450 kilograms) of grass seed.

The first attempts to restore natural vegetation to the land which Craigmont's operation disturbed began in 1969. The now-dormant open pit allowed the seeding of the waste dumps. As well, to improve stabilization, the completed portion of the face of the tailings dam was seeded. In both areas, the seed and the fertilizer were applied with an aircraft, a common method at the time due to its convenience, its ease of application and its expedience.

Use of the Merritt airport was impractical because of its distance from the site and the fact more than 50 trips would be needed to seed and to fertilize the planned 223 acres (90 hectares) of the first phase. An airstrip was built on a waste dump and all of the tailings dam and half the waste dumps were seeded using a special mixture of annual ryegrass, boreal fescue, crested wheatgrass, rhizoma alfalfa and other grasses.

Success Marginal at First

With the melting snow of the following spring, the piles of broken rock began to show a tinge of green. Additional fertilizer was spread in 1970; however, an abnormally dry summer set back the program.

Craigmont Pit — April 1983. Erosion is smoothing the contours and trees and shrubs are beginning to grow.

Murphy Shewchuk photo

Between 1969 and 1977, the reclamation program was only marginally successful due to a combination of factors. The semi-desert climate of the area was not conducive to aerial seeding or to fertilizing and the reclamation program remained a low-priority task in the minds of Craigmont management.

Farming Techniques Applied

In 1978, with the closure of the mine in sight, reclamation became a high-priority task. Lloyd Gavelin was placed in charge of the reclamation program with plans to seed the remaining pit areas.

Aerial seeding at the rate of 100 pounds per acre (112 kilograms per hectare) had been proposed. After studying the proposal, Gavelin suggested if the seed was covered only one quarter the amount of seed would be required and the whole operation would cost less than what was originally budgeted for seed.

Farm Tractor Used

"We went into partial seeding of some of the waste dumps to see how the ground method would work," said Gavelin. "We hooked a cyclone seed spreader and another cyclone fertilizer spreader on a farm tractor and dragged a chain harrows behind to mix the seed and the fertilizer into the top layer of soil."

"The areas where we started (seeding) were quite flat, except for the free dump area where we flattened out the waste rock with a Cat."

"We had to make sure there was moisture available to get the plants started," said Gavelin. "As soon as the snow left the ground and the ground was still soft was the best time to seed."

"The operation worked well. In many places, the alfalfa growth is waist high and it is now reseeding itself."

"We also brought in a contractor in 1978 and fenced off the pit area to keep the cattle out and to give the new growth a chance to become established. When the mine has been released of all its responsibility for the area, the Forest Service range management division will likely have to decide when to let the cattle back."

Reclamation Program to Continue

Bill Diment, mine manager at the time of the mine's shutdown suggested Lloyd Gavelin would probably continue to be involved with the reclamation program for up to five years after the remainder of the mine operation has ceased.

Reclamation of the mine site has also been undertaken in other forms. The land at the upper portals has been contoured and it covers the sealed mine openings so as to make them blend into the hillside. Buildings, equipment and power lines will be removed and the area will be left clean and orderly.

In the dry climate of the Nicola Valley, it may be decades before the scars of Craigmont disappear, but trees and grass are starting to grow where once "twenty-seven ton (24-tonne) 'Eucs' — Euclid dump trucks — whipped about like jeeps, their powerful diesels growling like angry lions."

Euclid #19 — September, 1970.

Craigmont photo

Industrial Relations

Craigmont Mines Ltd. began operation during the expansive period of the early 1960s when technology as we know it was just beginning to infiltrate the conservative mining industry. This time period also saw trade unions begin to flex their muscles on behalf of their members and to increase union membership in the work place. For the better part of the life of the Craigmont mine, industrial relations were a seesaw relationship between a strong management and a strong union.

Initial Agreement Promises Labor Stability

In May, 1961, as Craigmont neared the production stage of its operation, the company signed a four-year agreement with the Highland Valley and District Local 1011, International Union of Mine, Mill and Smelter Workers that promised labor stability until July 11, 1965.

Mine-Mill Rebels Seek Breakaway

"Application for a breakaway from Mine, Mill and Smelter Workers's Union has been filed by a group of workers at Craigmont."

"A source within the labor movement said the application is on behalf of a membership of more than 200 employed by Canadian Explorations Ltd."

"The spokesman said the dissenting group is 'fed up' with the union and its current contract.

"Mine-Mill has been described publicly in the past as a Red-led union. It was expelled from the Canadian Congress of Labor, predecessor to the Canadian Labor Congress, for alleged Communist leadership in 1953."

"Harvey Murphy, Western president of Mine-Mill, has consistently denied the accusation."

Mine-Mill Union Ousted

The United Steelworkers of America launched an offensive against the International Union of Mine, Mill and Smelter Workers at Craigmont early in 1963. Mine-Mill threw up legal barriers which blocked USWA's application for a certification vote with an injunction. However, the move proved to be of no avail. Through a government-conducted vote, the Steelworkers union won the right to represent Craigmont employees and was so certified in August, 1963.

Mine-Mill took legal proceedings which contested the certification and March 17, 1964, the certification of the USWA was set aside. Another government-supervised vote was taken and the Labour Relations Board, on April 15, 1964, again granted certification to Local 6523 of the United Steelworkers of America.

The 1965-1966 Strike

The labor agreement originally signed between Craigmont and Mine-Mill and inherited by the Steelworkers expired July 11, 1965. Steelworkers area supervisor Pen Baskin assisted Steelworkers Local 6523 acting-President James T. Rabbitt in bargaining. Baskin became the outspoken representative of the Craigmont workers.

The Steelworkers union demanded wage increases ranging from 55 to 102 per cent while the company offered 18 to 19 per cent. The union rejected the offer and held a strike vote September 28, 1965. Two days later, the pickets went up and Craigmont was shut down for the first time.

Toronto "Globe and Mail" reporter George McFarlane summed up the background to Craigmont's first labor strike this way in a 1966 story:

THE PROVINCE B.C.

Monday, June 10, 1968   ★★★13

Merritt warned of long strike

Mayor George Fillinger of Merritt says the two-day-old strike at nearby Craigmont Copper Mine could become a lon gone like the last "unless we do something right away."

The 350 miners at Craigmont, members of the Steelworkers Union, set up picket lines Saturday after rejecting a company offer of a 56-cent hourly increase in a 30-month contract.

"They (the company and workers) are close," said Mayor Fillinger Sunday. "It's just a matter of bringing them together. We haven't given up yet. But if we don't succeed in bringing them together quickly, this is going to be a long strike."

The mayor said Merritt doesn't want a repeat of the Craimont strike of two years ago which lasted over six months and virtually strangled the community economically.

The current contract at Craigmont expired last April. The union would like a two-year contract to give them a June, 1970, expiry date in common with the lumber industry and many mining operations.

"This would give us an opportunity to bargain on a common wage pattern," said union staff representative Monty Alton.

Alton said he expects an answer from Labor Minister Peterson for the appointment of an industrial inquiry commissioner after the cabinet meets Tuesday.

It was a commissioner who settled the last strike at Craigmont.

Present mine rates are $2.45 an hour for laborers and $3.40 for tradesmen.

"The struggle goes far beyond a simple contract disagreement between Craigmont workers and management."

"The Steelworkers's union is working toward its first contract at Craigmont, having ousted Mine, Mill and Smelter Workers, and it seems determined to set a new wage pattern in the industry. Its demands have been far above anything paid in British Columbia and it has been encouraged recently by the marked success of its first British Columbia contract negotiation at Cassiar Asbestos Corp. Ltd., near the Yukon border."

"Craigmont management seems equally determined to resist the powerful newcomer to the industry, claiming to be the victim of a union power struggle. It has agreed, however, that its last agreement (with Mine-Mill) needed sharp upward revision in favor of the employees. It has offered what amounted to a 15 per cent wage increase and has made a succession of slightly better offers, each rejected by the union."

After three months of negotiations, Labor Minister Leslie Peterson appointed Mr. Justice Victor Dryer of the B.C. Supreme Court as an Industrial Inquiry Commissioner on January 1, 1966 to help settle the dispute. Negotiations continued under Dryer's supervision until April 18, 1966, when the signing of a two-year contract gave the Steelworkers wage increases ranging from 35 to 40 per cent over the life of the agreement. In the process, Justice Dryer rewrote the Craigmont-Steelworkers contract and in doing so, he created a master agreement that was followed elsewhere in the mining industry.

"This contract was by far the best in Western Canada," said James Rabbitt. "Within a year, most contracts in the mining industry had been reopened and wages established at Craigmont became the norm."

1968 Strike

Negotiations for a new labor contract began in March, 1968, amid unsettled provincial labor conditions. Steelworkers Local President Jack Diamond was determined to get a favorable contract for his membership. Management was equally determined not to set an industry precedent. Wages and shiftwork were the major points of contention. After hard bargaining and a nine-day strike, June 8 to 16, an agreement was reached which provided a 56-cent-an-hour increase over a 27-month period.

Amicable Negotiations

In September, 1970, Craigmont and the United Steelworkers signed an agreement which covered wages and working conditions until September 16, 1972. In a year of much labor strife in British Columbia, the fact the new contract was signed three weeks prior to the expiry of the previous agreement was a major accomplishment.

During 1971, negotiations began on severance and retirement plans which were intended to create a means of assisting employees to relocate in order to find new employment in the event of the closure of the mine.

Negotiations in 1972 resulted in a one-year agreement with an average increase of eight per cent which brought the average annual wage of a Craigmont employee up to $10,349.

Second Longest Strike

With Robert Baird as local union president and Tony Petrina as Craigmont mine manager, 1973 contract negotiations became an exercise in confrontation. The strike began September 16, 1973, when workers walked off the job during contract negotiations. Union members turned down the company offer and then walked off the job after a company supervisor confronted them. Charges and counter-charges of an illegal lockout and/or strike persisted for a month before the parties returned to the bargaining table. Negotiations continued in a series of stops and starts until they completely bogged down in early December.

Frustrated with the whole negotiating procedure, the union considered asking NDP Premier Dave Barrett to have the government take over the mine and operate it for the remainder of its life.

In late January, both sides agreed to binding arbitration as a way out of the continuing stalemate. Industrial Inquiry Commissioner Jack Sherlock quickly brought the two parties together and hammered out an agreement.

A story in the Wednesday, February 6, 1974, issue of the Merritt Herald proclaimed the end of the second longest strike in Craigmont's 15-year history.

Craigmont Miners Return as Highest Paid in B.C.

Darwin T. Benson, USWA district representative, praised the new agreement:

"The Union (did not) get all (its) contract demands, but the contract is certainly acceptable, and is one of the top agreements in the Mining Industry in British Columbia, exceeding the recent Similkameen and Bethlehem Copper agreements."

72

Craigmont President Ross G. Duthie was not impressed with the settlement:

"The agreement awarded the employees an increase of 40 per cent (on) the base wage in a 16-month period for a contract of two year duration."

"It is a binding decision. We are stuck with it, the Unions are stuck with it and the public is stuck with it. Craigmont is now one of the highest, if not THE highest, paying mine in the world!"

"Such wage guidelines, plus the consistent rumored increases of taxes, new royalties, etc., cannot but deter further investments in the basic industries of this Province."

Agreements were negotiated in 1976, 1977, 1979 and 1981 with an increased emphasis placed on relocation and severance as Craigmont's mining operation neared its end. By 1979, the average income per employee, including benefits, had risen to $19,970. Further negotiations raised this average income to $26,930 in 1981. As well, the completion bonus reached $1.00 per hour worked for each employee who remained at his job until his last scheduled shift ended.

Craigmont Apprenticeship Program

A training program is important in any industry that employs skilled tradesmen. The apprenticeship program, as it existed at Craigmont, was based on the Apprenticeship Act which the British Columbia government passed in 1935. Craigmont's apprentices were initially placed on a three-month trial before a Contract of Apprenticeship, which set out the conditions of employment, was signed. In addition to on-the-job training, apprentices were required to attend day-school classes away from home. Craigmont apprentices received full wages while they attended classes.

Apprenticeships were offered in a variety of trades, including machinists, electricians, millwrights, heavy-duty mechanics, welders and automotive mechanics.

The first apprentice was indentured as a steel fabricator in 1961. A total of 109 apprentices were indentured at Craigmont; a total of 52 of them completed their training at the mine. The largest number of apprentices were heavy-duty mechanics, followed closely by industrial electricians.

Bob Baird was one of the many Craigmont employees who took advantage of the apprenticeship program. Baird started working for Craigmont in the open-pit operation in 1966 as a blasthole driller's helper after a varied career that included service with the Armed Forces, surveying and diamond-drilling. Baird worked in the open pit until the last of the cleanup was completed in 1967 before he was transferred underground as a laborer. He quickly moved up to the nipper's job and then became king nipper.

"I think the king nipper name came from Salmo," said Bob Baird. "The king nipper was the guy who had to get the wedges, drill bits, blasting powder and stuff like that and take it into the mine while at the same time dodging ore trains and crew trains."

Baird's electronic training in the Royal Canadian Air Force gave him a two-and-one-half-year credit when he applied for his electrician's apprenticeship. He completed his apprenticeship with Craigmont in October, 1971. While serving his apprenticeship, he became interested in Steelworkers union activities and he quickly became president of Local 6523. Baird also served as an alderman on Merritt City Council and as mayor during the late 1970s and the early 1980s.

Student Employment Program

Craigmont had an active student employment program from the start of production in 1961.

"Placer Development policy, in which Craigmont participated, was to make recruiting trips each spring to all major Canadian universities," said Bill Diment.

"Emphasis was placed on second and third-year students in engineering disciplines pertinent to mining. During these students's penultimate year, we assessed them and offered the successful candidates permanent employment after graduation."

"High-school students were also hired to give them some exposure to mining in the hope it may influence them to pursue mining disciplines after graduation."

Students were employed to replace vacationing employees in both the surface and the underground operations based on the estimate that the majority of the work force would take vacations at some point during the summer months. Rather than shut down operations for a fixed vacation period, Craigmont management went the route of staggered vacations because it was felt employing students provided them with financial assistance as well as practical experience and an introduction to the mining environment.

Bill Diment, the man assigned the task of closing Craigmont after 20 years of operation. October, 1982.

Murphy Shewchuk photo

Safety First

There is little doubt mining can be a hazardous industry, but in order to minimize the hazard and to keep safety foremost in the minds of the work force, first aid and mine rescue training were important parts of mining life. First-aid attendants were on staff at the mine and first-aid courses were offered to all personnel. Mine rescue training involved teamwork; Craigmont's mine rescue team often placed well in competitions between British Columbia mines. In competitions which the British Columbia Department of Mines sponsored, the teams were required to rescue personnel involved in a simulated industrial accident. The teams were judged on the basis of their proficiency in rescue skills and in first aid work.

Open-Pit Mine Rescue Competitions

The first annual Provincial Surface Mine Rescue Competition was held at the Craigmont mine October 5, 1974. This competition was the first surface provincial final championship to be held in British Columbia. The competing teams were from Gibraltar Mines near Williams Lake and Brenda Mines near Peachland. Although Craigmont was not among the finalists, the open pit was used because it was no longer being actively mined.

During 1982, its last year of operation, Craigmont was the winner of the regional John T. Ryan Safety Award for the mine with the lowest accident frequency — a real accomplishment considering the hazards of shutting down the mine.

Joint Relocation Program

As it became clearer no new ore existed in the Craigmont deposit and the mine would soon be closed, the company and the union established a joint union-management employment assistance program to aid in finding continued employment for those workers laid off as a result of reduced work. The first application of this program came in the fall of 1981 when 34 men were laid off. By the time production ended in 1982, 62 per cent of those people who sought assistance had found employment.

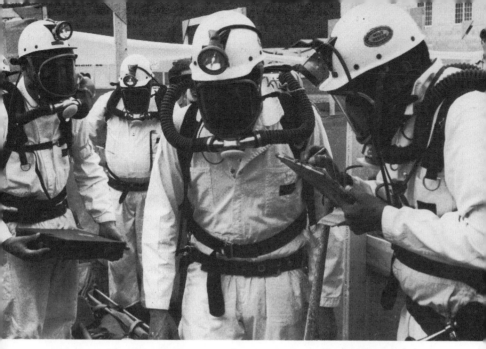

Industrial relations emphasize safety first at mine rescue competitions — June 1971.

Craigmont photo

"We did not need to lay many people off," said Bill Diment, mine manager during the last years of Craigmont's operation. "I think, in hindsight, having the scare of an early closure helped us tremendously. At the time I made the first announcement of closure, there were approximately 350 people on payroll. As the operation wound down, attrition took care of the necessary reductions. Fortunately, this attrition carried right through until the fall of 1981 when we had our first layoffs."

"As part of the assistance program, we sent out a skills inventory to all of the major industries in British Columbia. It was through their interest that they came in for on-site interviews with our people. Some seven mining companies interviewed our workers."

On December 31, 1982, 37 hourly-paid employees were laid off at Craigmont which ended an era for the Nicola Valley and a mining operation that had begun more than two decades earlier. Except for a few salaried personnel involved with disposing the equipment and the half-million (450,000 tonnes) of stockpiled magnetite, Craigmont was finished.

Community Relations

Tremendous Impact on Merritt

The discovery of copper on the slopes of the Promontory Hills and the development of Craigmont had a tremendous impact on the nearby town of Merritt. In 1955, the population of this frontier-style community was about 1,700 people. By 1968, when Craigmont's employment peaked at 660, Merritt's population was up to 5,500. With the boom came prosperity, a novel state for a community that went bankrupt during the Depression. Stores, supermarkets, restaurants, garages and hotels blossomed as they were nourished with an annual payroll that reached $7,193,000 in 1977.

Helped Establish Bench Subdivision

While Craigmont did not establish company housing, as was often the practice in other mining communities, it did support Merritt in establishing the Bench subdivision. Craigmont purchased a number of unserviced lots for $10,000 cash which provided the municipality with the seed money needed to service the subdivision and to sell lots on which government approved National Housing Association (NHA) homes could be built. This action, in turn, stimulated a number of private developers to create other subdivisions within Merritt's boundaries.

Tony Petrina was one of the employees who bought a lot in the Bench subdivision and built his own home. Tony's wife, Gloria, preferred the atmosphere in Merritt compared to company towns in which she had lived in the past.

Merritt Offered Amenities to Miners

Generally, Merritt offered a choice of recreational amenities as well as schools and churches. Merritt was a regular stop on the Overture Concert circuit in the early 1960s. The local drama club received strong support as it filled the cultural gap between concert performances. The community had an ice arena and a curling club for winter recreation.

"What I liked about Merritt was my friends came from all walks of life," said Gloria Petrina. "You can get pretty boxed in if everything you do is with the same people."

Craigmont Supported New Hospital

A new hospital was built in Merritt during the summer of 1963 and the new company on the Promontory Hills donated more than $17,000 toward purchase of an X-ray machine and other equipment. In addition, the company gave financial assistance to the community tennis courts, swimming pool, arena and public library.

Employees Participate in Civic Politics

The Craigmont employees and their families quickly became an integral part of the community. The men played an active part in

Craigmont Sponsored team —1977.

Starlite Studio photo

local politics as they served on library, hospital and school boards and on Merritt council. Craigmont electrician Bob Baird served as mayor in 1979 and 1980. Former Craigmont employee Jim Rabbitt served as an alderman on Merritt Council for six years, from 1969 to 1974, and he later took over the mayor's chair from Baird.

"The company supported the efforts of its employees to the extent they wanted to get involved with the affairs of the community," said Tony Petrina. "Craigmont was a contributor when the new hospital was built and when the swimming pool and the tennis courts were started, but none of the contributions were major."

Mayor Allan Collett (l) accepts $10,000 cheque from Bill Diment, Mgr. Craigmont Mines, Feb. 1977 for recreation improvements to Nicola Valley in Merritt. February, 1977.

Mayor of Merritt James T. Rabbitt.

Vancouver Sun photo

Company Supported Extended Care Residence

Craigmont made one of the largest, if not the largest, private donations to the construction of Coquihalla House, an intermediate-care residence built in Merritt in 1981. Craigmont's donation of $80,000 helped the Coquihalla Community Care Society provide additional furnishings and a quiet room for the residents. In honor of Craigmont and the part it played in the community, the additional room was named the Craigmont Room.

CRAIGMONT MINES LIMITED

19 January 1981

Mr. Ted Kampa
Chairman
Coquihalla Community Care Society
P.O. Box 129
Merritt, BC
VOK 2B0

Dear Mr. Kampa:

On behalf of Craigmont Mines and its Board of Directors, I am pleased to forward to the Coquihalla Community Care Society a cheque for $80,000 as a donation towards the construction and furnishing of your Intermediate Care facility in Merritt.

$50,000 is to go towards the construction and furnishing of a "Quiet Room" within the facility. The Board of Directors wishes this portion of the donation to be recognized by the society by some appropriate display means to commemorate the many contributions the employees of Craigmont Mines have made to the well being of Merritt.

The remaining $30,000 is to go towards the society's "Fund Raising Campaign" to assist in covering the extra costs the society deems necessary in improving the Standard of the Coquihalla House.

It is a pleasure to become a contributor towards the development of such a worthwhile facility. My very best to you and the board members in achieving your goals in the development of Coquihalla House.

Yours truly,

CRAIGMONT MINES LIMITED

W.D. Diment

W.D. Diment
Mine Manager

Lucile McDiarmid opens Craigmont display at Nicola Valley Museum Archives, May 1, 1983.

Merritt Herald photo

History Recorded and Displayed

As Craigmont's life as a copper mine in the Nicola Valley drew to a close, Mine Manager Bill Diment became interested in seeing the history of the operation preserved in the form of a written work and displays at the Nicola Valley Museum-Archives in Merritt and the British Columbia Museum of Mining at Britannia Beach near Squamish, British Columbia. The result is this written history and displays of graphics and artifacts at both locations.

Student Scholarships

Craigmont began offering scholarships to graduates of Merritt Secondary School in 1970. The first award established was in the form of four installments of $500. In order to receive the full amount, the winner was required to enroll in a four-year program leading to a Bachelor's degree from a recognized Canadian university.

In 1971, two additional scholarships were awarded to graduates of Merritt Secondary School. These two scholarships were provided for students at the British Columbia Institute of Technology in Burnaby, British Columbia. In 1972, a total of $3,200 in scholarships were awarded.

Craigmont continued the scholarship program throughout the life of the mine and gradually expanded the program until the company awarded $5,000 per year to worthy students during the latter years of operation.

School District No. 31 (Merritt)
Merritt, B.C.

1983 03 15

Craigmont Mines Limited,
P.O. Box 3000,
MERRITT, B. C.
VOK 2B0

Attention: Mr. Bill Diment

Dear Sir:

On behalf of the Board of School Trustees, School District No. 31 (MERRITT), I would like to thank Craigmont Mines Limited for their support during their years in Merritt. At the school level, scholarships, mine tours as well as equipment and supply donations have been extremely beneficial to students.

At the district level, Mr. A.J. Petrina, Mr. J. Thompson, Mr. C. Rennie and Mr. H. Peters all served on the Merritt School Board. As Board members, these individuals helped shape the educational system in Merritt.

Craigmont Mines Limited set an example of a corporate citizen that will be difficult for other companies to follow. Your company will definitely be missed in Merritt.

Yours truly,

E.A. Reimer,
Chairman of the Board

EAR/sp

pc: Placer Developments Limited

Personality Profiles

Records suggest as many as 5,000 people worked for Craigmont Mines Ltd. between the conception of the company in 1951 and the cessation of mining operations at the end of 1982. Therefore, the following list of "personalities" is little more than a random selection of people with colorful and varied backgrounds who contributed to the operation of the company and, while doing so, helped to enrich the greater community of man. The author extends his apologies to the thousands of people who have been overlooked because of lack of space. Their contribution has not been forgotten.

Neil McDiarmid — founder and director of Craigmont Mines Ltd.
Photo courtesy Lucile McDiarmid.

Neil H. McDiarmid:
Barrister and Solicitor

Neil H. McDiarmid was a lawyer with his heart in British Columbia's mining industry. McDiarmid was born in 1896 in Lindsay, Ontario, and he came to British Columbia in 1912. A veteran of World War One, McDiarmid served as a pilot in the Royal Flying Corp during which time he barely survived after he was shot down over the North Sea. He completed his legal training after the war and he set up a law practice in British Columbia's Cariboo during the early 1920s while he lived first in Likely and then in Williams Lake.

McDiarmid's first clients were mining companies involved in reworking the old placer gold diggings that had attracted thousands of miners during the 1860s. It may have been during this time "gold fever" infected McDiarmid with a lifelong interest in mining.

In 1929, McDiarmid, his wife Lucile and their two children, moved to Vancouver and he set up an office in the Williams Building where he practised patent law.

Law may have been McDiarmid's bread and butter, but the perpetual optimist in him shone through as his heart was in mining. At various times, his mining interests took him to the Bridge River Valley, the Kettle Valley and the Similkameen region with varied degrees of success. When the Highland Valley copper boom started in the early 1950s, Craigmont Mines Ltd. and Neil H. McDiarmid were ready for action.

McDiarmid just missed participating in the development of Bethlehem Copper, but he did succeed in turning a copper-iron orebody on the slopes of the Promontory Hills into British Columbia's first large-scale open-pit copper mine.

His perserverance and effort, particularly in the pre-production years, were instrumental in bringing the mine into successful operation.

Neil Howard McDiarmid served on the Craigmont board of directors until his death February 27, 1972, at the age of 75.

Harry Merrell (l) — September, 1971.

Merritt Herald photo

Harry Merrell: Prospector

Harry Merrell was born in Carnduff, Northwest Territories (now Saskatchewan) in 1900. Merrell first developed an interest in prospecting when he was 18 while he worked for a diamond drilling outfit. His interest continued and he took part in claim-staking rushes in Northern Saskatchewan as well as many parts of British Columbia, including the Fort Nelson area in the 1940s and the Queen Charlotte Islands in the 1950s.

Harry Merrell was working for Neil H. McDiarmid and Craigmont in the Jackson Lake area of the Promontory Hills in 1954 when he staked the claims that now cover Craigmont's open pit. He was based in Chilliwack at the time, but he later moved to Merritt where he worked as an exploration and construction contractor.

While he worked for Egil Lorntzsen in 1964, Merrell helped uncover the discovery showing at the giant Lornex copper mine in the Highland Valley.

On September 1, 1971, Harry Merrell had the honor of registering the 50,000th mining claim in the Nicola Mining Division. In the summer of 1982, Merrell was still active and doing some prospecting from a home base in North Bend, Washington.

John D. Simpson: Engineer

John D. Simpson was born in 1901, in Tasmania, Australia. He received his education in Australia and, after he earned his engineering degree, his employer, the Electrolytic Zinc Company, sent him to Europe in 1923 "for experience."

After 18 months, Simpson was offered a job in Chile, where he worked until 1927, before he took a job in the Peruvian Andes. He met his future wife at Aroyo, Peru, where she worked as an American nurse. After a 4,000-mile (6,500-kilometre) trip down the Amazon River, a short stay in the United States and a stint with the MacIntyre Mine near Timmins, Ontario, Simpson began working for Yukon Consolidated Gold in Dawson City, Yukon.

After five years in the Yukon, John Simpson was offered a job with Placer Development as assistant manager of its gold dredging operation in Colombia, South America. From Colombia, Simpson was assigned the job of assistant manager of Placer's Bulolo gold dredging operation in New Guinea, an island north of Australia.

Simpson arrived in Bulolo in 1940 and he was forced to shut down operations in 1941 when the Japanese overran the area. He joined the Australian army as a captain during the New Guinea campaign and he later served in the ministry of munitions.

After the war, Simpson went back to New Guinea as manager of Bulolo. In 1949, he was transferred to Vancouver as vice-president of Placer. He later succeeded Charles Banks as president of Placer Development Ltd.

John Simpson's association with Craigmont began during the initial exploration stage in 1958. He was elected a director of the company in 1960 and he was appointed president in 1961 when he guided Craigmont through the development and the construction stages. Simpson retired in 1968 and Ross G. Duthie replaced him as president of Craigmont.

John D. Simpson.

John Roberts: Miner

John Roberts was born September 11, 1925, at Greenway, Manitoba, where he began his education.

"I did not go to school for long," said Roberts. "I only made it to grade four. Then I worked on the farms until 1948, except for one year in the army during the war. I started mining gold at Snow Lake, Manitoba. I worked tramming mostly, then I went on the shaft crew. I worked there for four years before I moved.

"I stuck to mining and I went to Yellowknife where I worked at the Giant Yellowknife mine. I did not stay there long — only six months. It was too cold. I had to get out of there."

Roberts moved south to the Canex-Placer operation in Salmo, British Columbia, where he worked for six years. During his first year in Salmo, Roberts met and married his wife, Marion.

Underground mining — John Roberts.

Craigmont photo

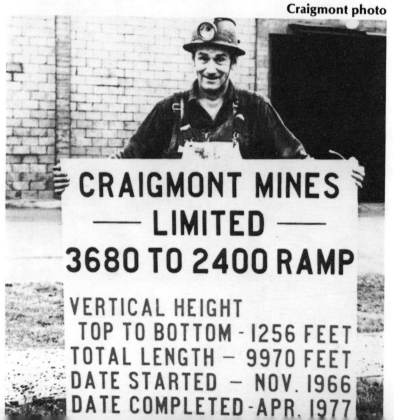

CRAIGMONT MINES
— LIMITED —
3680 TO 2400 RAMP
VERTICAL HEIGHT
TOP TO BOTTOM - 1256 FEET
TOTAL LENGTH — 9970 FEET
DATE STARTED — NOV. 1966
DATE COMPLETED - APR. 1977

Placer transferred Roberts to Craigmont in August, 1958, as one of Craigmont's first underground miners.

"I started at the 3,500-foot (1,601-metre) level," said Roberts. "I started as a miner drilling, blasting and mucking out the ore or the waste. We put in timber too, but the ground was pretty bad there."

"I worked underground all the time except for three months of drilling and blasting in the open pit."

"When they finished working the open pit, we started at the 3,500-foot (1,601-metre) level and we drove a tunnel right up into the floor of the pit."

Just about all of John Roberts's work at Craigmont involved development mining as he initially helped to prepare the way for further exploration. He helped to prepare the sublevel caving operation in later years.

In 1977, John Roberts received a silver platter in honor of 25 years service with Placer Development.

Roberts was also one of Craigmont's most senior miners. In addition to starting the underground operation, he helped to end it as he drilled the last drift round at Craigmont early in 1982.

Roberts was laid off at the end of April, 1982, but he started work two weeks later with the Goldstream Division of Noranda Mines Ltd., a new base-metal mine north of Revelstoke, British Columbia.

On January 11, 1983, while working at the Goldstream operation, John Roberts became a member of the Turtle Club, an honor which the British Columbia Safety Council bestows on those people whose hard hats have prevented them from suffering serious injury or death. Roberts says a 100-pound (45-kilogram) chunk of rock glanced off his hat, struck his shoulder and cut through his boot.

Despite this accident and another accident in 1975, when an air hose blew and knocked Roberts off a ladder — he suffered a broken leg — he still considers a mine a safe place to work.

"It is no more dangerous than working in a sawmill. The only thing you really have to worry about is loose rock. I would sooner work underground than anywhere else."

91

Ross G. Duthie: Engineer

Born in 1920 in Winnipeg, Manitoba, Ross Duthie entered the University of Manitoba before he enlisted in the Canadian infantry during World War Two. After the war, Duthie resumed his education and he graduated with a Bachelor of Arts and Sciences degree in mining from the University of British Columbia before he worked for Cominco at Sullivan and Riondel for three years. He joined the Placer group as a metallurgist in the Salmo lead-zinc concentrator and he served as manager of Craigmont from 1958 to 1964 during development of the mine and its early years of operation.

Duthie turned over the reins at Craigmont and he became closely involved with Placer's Gibraltar, Endako and Marcopper mines as he spent several months in Manila as project manager of the latter mine.

Ross Duthie was named president of Craigmont Mines Ltd. July 1, 1967, while he retained his position as assistant to the president of Placer Development Ltd.

Duthie was elected president and chief executive officer of Placer Development in April, 1975, as he succeeded Thomas H. McClelland.

Duthie retired as president of Placer Development in July, 1981, and C. Allen Born succeeded him.

President and Chief Executive Officer of Placer Mines Ross G. Duthie.

Williams Bros. photo

Anthony J. Petrina — Senior Vice President Placer Mines, President Craigmont Mines Ltd.

Williams Bros. photo

Anthony J. (Tony) Petrina: Mining Engineer

Born in Sudbury, Ontario, Tony Petrina is a graduate in mining engineering from Queens University in Kingston, Ontario. Prior to joining Craigmont Mines in 1960, Petrina worked for a wide variety of mines in eastern Canada, including International Nickel and Falconbridge Nickel Mines Ltd.

Tony Petrina started with Craigmont as an underground mine engineer. He later became underground mine superintendent and he was appointed mine manager in 1968. He held this position until January, 1974, when he accepted the post of vice-president, operations, with the Placer group; E.W. Cockayne replaced Petrina as mine manager. In November, 1981, Petrina was appointed president of Craigmont Mines Ltd.

Robert Baird: Electrician

Robert Baird was born in Vernon, British Columbia in 1940.

He served in the Royal Canadian Air Force (RCAF) from 1958 to 1961 as a radar technician and a pilot in the CF104 program. After he left the RCAF, Baird worked as a surveyor and a diamond-driller as he did exploration work in various parts of the Nicola Valley, including the Craigmont claims.

Baird began working for Craigmont in 1966 during the last stages of the open-pit mining operation. His first job was as a driller's helper on the 40R as he drilled nine-inch (22-centimetre) diameter holes into the orebody which were later filled with explosives and detonated to break loose the ore. When the open-pit cleanup was completed, Baird was transferred underground where he worked his way through a variety of trades. He received his journeyman certificate as an electrician in 1971.

Baird became interested in union activities in 1968 and he was elected recording secretary of Local 6523 of the United Steelworkers of America that same year. In 1969, Baird was elected president of Local 6523, a position he held until the mine ceased all operations at the end of 1982.

Baird first ran for Merritt Town Council in 1972, but he lost to incumbent Alderman Jim Rabbitt, a former Craigmont employee, by five votes. He ran again in 1973 and this time he was elected to the position of alderman. Baird was appointed interim-mayor in February, 1979, and he was elected to the position in August, 1979. He served the remainder of his term, but Rabbitt defeated him in the fall elections in 1980.

Local 6523 United Steel Workers of America President Robert Baird. **Vancouver Sun photo**

Lloyd Gavelin: Agrologist

Lloyd Gavelin started his life in the mining community of Bralorne, British Columbia, in 1942 before he moved to a ranch in the Nicola Valley with his parents in 1945. After he received his early education in the Nicola Valley, Gavelin moved on to the University of British Columbia where he got his Bachelor of Science degree in agriculture in 1967.

Lloyd Gavelin August, 1982.

Murphy Shewchuk photo

During his university years, Gavelin worked at various summer jobs at Craigmont, including pit serviceman, truck driver and security guard. After graduation, his hopes of getting into the ranching business did not work out and he returned to the mine as an underground laborer. Gavelin quickly worked his way up from laborer to long-hole blaster and then to shift boss in the Number One East orebody. He later became involved with a job standards program aimed at improving mine productivity.

In 1978, Gavelin returned to the agriculture field when he was given the task of carrying on Craigmont's reclamation program. Some of the reclamation methods he introduced at Craigmont have been adopted elsewhere in the mining industry.

William D. "Bill" Diment: Mining Engineer

Bill Diment came from a mining background. He was born in Dawson City, Yukon, in 1937 and he was raised in that northern mining community. During his early years of university education, Diment worked for United Keno Hill Mines as a summer student.

In 1962, Diment graduated as a mining engineer from the University of British Columbia and he went to work for the Giant Yellowknife Mines in the Northwest Territories. After two and one half years, Diment and his wife moved to the Lake Dufault mine in Noranda, Quebec. During this period of time, he had worked his way up from engineer-in-training to general superintendent. Early in 1969, Diment moved to the New Quebec Raglan project in the eastern Arctic to become resident project manager.

After a short stint with a contractor in Sudbury, Ontario, Diment moved to the newly-opened Gibraltar Mine near Williams Lake, British Columbia, where he worked his way up to pit superintendent.

Bill Diment began working at Craigmont as mine manager in October, 1976, with the clear understanding he would likely be the man responsible for shutting down the operation.

"Mr. Petrina told me at the time it had some two or three years to go and it was his wish, as well as everyone else's, that it be done in an amicable and a thorough manner."

With the aid of market conditions, an able workforce and the utilization of what was originally considered "waste," Diment was able to extend the life of Craigmont for six years before mining operations were completed in 1982.

Craigmont Mine Managers

1958 to November 1, 1964	Ross G. Duthie
November 1, 1964 to 1968	R. E. Hallbauer
1968 to January, 1974	A. J. Petrina
January 1974 to January, 1977	E. W. Cokayne
January 1977 to 1983	W. D. Diment

William D. "Bill' Diment October, 1982.
Murphy Shewchuk photo

Glossary of Mining Terms

Anomaly:

A deviation from the norm in rock patterns which is usually discovered through geophysical methods. An anomaly suggests the possibility of a mineral deposit, but only one in thousands of anomalies ever leads to a worthwhile mineral discovery.

Anticline:

An arch or a fold in the layers of rock shaped like the crest of a wave.

Assay:

The testing of a sample of minerals or ore to determine its content of valuable minerals.

Ball Mill:

A piece of milling equipment used to grind ore into small particles. This milling equipment uses steel balls as the grinding medium inside a rotating drum.

Bedrock:

The solid rock of the earth's crust which is generally covered with overburden of soil or water.

Claim:

An area of land or water which a prospector or a mining organization "claims" for the purpose of exploring the claim for a certain length of time and subject to certain conditions. Claims are first staked out and then they are recorded in a government claim-recording office. A common size of a claim in Canada is about 40 acres (16 hectares).

Concentrate:

To treat ore so the resulting substance contains a lower amount of the waste and a higher amount of the valuable mineral. The concentrate is then smelted and refined to obtain the pure metal.

Core:

A cylindrical piece of rock that a diamond drill extracts from the earth.

Development:

To bring a mining property to the production stage.

Diamond Drilling:

The extreme hardness of the diamonds enables the diamond-faced drill bit to cut through all rocks and all minerals found in the earth's crust. Hollow steel rods connect the bit to the driving machinery. Inside the first rod is a core barrel that holds the core of rock as the rotating drill bit advances.

At frequent intervals, the core is retrieved and stored in special boxes for future examination. The interesting sections of the core are split lengthwise and one half is retained for a permanent record while the other half is sent to an assayer for an analysis.

Fault:

A break in the earth's crust. Ore deposits are commonly associated with faults because the movement frequently provides a channel for the passage of ore-bearing solutions.

Flotation:

A common milling process in which certain minerals in solution attach themselves to bubbles and float to the surface while others (less valuable) sink to the bottom and thus cause separation.

Gangue:

The worthless minerals associated with valuable minerals in an ore deposit.

Level:

A horizontal passage or tunnel in a mine; it is customary to establish levels at regular intervals while working mines.

Magnetometer:

A precision instrument capable of measuring small variations in the earth's magnetic field. The magnetometer is similar to a compass, except instead of pointing north, its needle points to a magnetic value proportional to the earth's magnetic field. This magnetic field varies and these variations can give geologists clues to mineral structures that lie beneath the surface of the earth.

Mill:

A plant, usually at the mine site, which concentrates ore in preparation for the ultimate recovery of the mineral in its pure form. A mill may also be the machine that grinds the ore to the proper size for further treatment.

Mineral:

A substance, which may or may not be of economic value, that naturally occurs in the earth. It is usually homogeneous, has a certain chemical makeup and usually appears in crystal or grain form.

Muck:

Ore or rock that has been broken through blasting.

Option:

A right to have the first chance to buy or to refuse to buy a mining claim or a group of claims.

Ore:

A mixture of minerals and gangue from which at least one of the minerals can be extracted at a profit.

Outcrop:

Solid rock or mineral that is exposed on the earth's surface and can be visually examined.

Overburden:

Soil, plant life or water that covers the earth's rock.

Placer:

A sand and gravel deposit which contains valuable minerals such as gold or platinum. A placer is an alluvial mineral deposit — that is, one which water action laid down. Placer mining is the technique used for the extraction of the mineral. The most common extraction method is dredging the material and concentrating it by sluicing it with water.

Prospect:

A mining property, the value of which has not been proved through exploration.

Raise:

A vertical or inclined underground tunnel that has been excavated from the bottom to the top.

Recovery:

The amount of mineral in ore that is separated in a mill.

Refining:

The final purification process of a metal or a mineral.

Rock:

Any naturally-formed combination of minerals which constitutes an appreciable part of the earth's crust.

Shaft:

An opening cut downward from the surface for transportation or ventilation purposes. It may be equipped with a hoist for raising or for lowering personnel or materials.

Staking:

To measure an area and to mark it with stakes or posts in order to establish mineral rights.

Stope:

An underground opening in which ore or waste is blasted and is broken.

Strip:

To remove the overburden which covers an orebody.

Tailings:

Waste material from a mineral-processing mill.

Waste:

Material that is too low in grade to be of economic value.

Bibliography and Sources

Newspapers and Magazines

Author/Editor	Source	Date
The Editors	Canadian Mining Journal	Various
Annual Reports	Craigmont Mines Ltd.	1957-1982
Beverly Dalton	The Daily Sentinel (Kamloops)	Dec. 16, 1979
Clayton Sinclair	FINANCIAL TIMES of Canada	Jan. 16-22/78
The Editors	Western Miner Magazine	Aug., 1976
The Editors	MINING: What mining means to Canada.	Sept., 1981
The Editors	The Pacific Miner	Sept. 28, 1961
Ron Renshaw	The Pacific Miner	April 12, 1982
The Editors	The Merritt Herald	Various
Various	The Vancouver Sun	Various

Personal and Telephone Interviews

Sherwin Kelly	Telephone Interview	July 29, 1982
Andre Orbeliani	Personal Interview	Aug. 1982
A.J. Petrina	Personal Interview	Aug. 8, 1982
Harry Merrell	Telephone Interview	Aug. 17, 1982
"Jack" Stinson	Telephone Interview	Aug. 20, 1982
Lloyd Gavelin	Personal Interview	Aug. 26, 1982
John D. Simpson	Personal Interview	Aug. 26, 1982
W.D. Diment	Personal Interview	Oct. 4, 1982
Lucile McDiarmid	Personal Interview	Nov. 13, 1982
Anthony Arnold	Telephone Interview	Nov. 16, 1982
Robert Baird	Personal Interview	Nov. 28, 1982
Ron Renshaw	Personal Interview	April, 1983
James Rabbitt	Personal Interview	April, 1983
John Roberts	Personal Interview	May 22, 1983

About the Author

Murphy Orlando Shewchuk was born in Hamilton, Ontario, September 14, 1943. He received his primary education in a rural school in central Saskatchewan and he completed his secondary education in the mining town of Bralorne, British Columbia. After he graduated in 1961, he worked in the gold mines before he joined the RCAF where he completed his training in communications and in electronics.

His first magazine articles were of a technical nature and they appeared in *Canadian ELECTRON* in the mid-1960s. While working at Shalalth, Shewchuk was a frequent contributor to Margaret "Ma" Murray's *Bridge River-Lillooet News*. In 1971, he moved to Kamloops and began writing a weekly *Outdoor Scene* column for the *Kamloops Daily Sentinel*. This column was continuously published for almost four years.

Since 1972, more than 200 of Shewchuk's magazine articles and/or photographs have appeared in such publications as *Alberta Motorist, BC Outdoors, Beautiful British Columbia, Camping Canada, Canadian Geographic, Outdoor Canada, The Writer, Westworld, Adventure Travel, Skyword, Western Living* and many others.

Shewchuk began writing books in 1973 with *Exploring Kamloops Country*, a backroads guide to the Kamloops region. In 1975, Hancock House published his second book, *Fur, Gold and Opals*. In 1980, he wrote the text for a 36-page special for Tourism British Columbia entitled *"Cariboo."* His most recent book, *Exploring the Nicola Valley*, was published in 1981 by Douglas and McIntyre of Vancouver. In all of these, he wrote the text, created the maps and took all the photographs.

His writing and his photography have received awards from the Outdoor Writers of Canada and the Macmillan Bloedel newspaper journalism competitions.

Shewchuk presently directs most of his writing energy to books and to magazine articles which deal with the outdoors. He enjoys digging for historical points of interest and he has an active interest in the background of British Columbia's mining industry.

Index